1998 EDITION

201 *Easy* Ways

TO

REDUCE *YOUR* TAXES

EVELYN JACKS

McGraw-Hill
Ryerson

Toronto   New York   Burr Ridge   Bangkok   Bogotá
Caracas   Lisbon   London   Madrid
Mexico City   Milan   Singapore   Sydney   Seoul   Taipei

McGraw-Hill
Ryerson Limited

A Subsidiary of The McGraw-Hill Companies

300 Water Street, Whitby, Ontario, L1N 9B6
http://www.mcgrawhill.ca

201 Easy Ways to Reduce Your Taxes

ISBN: 0-07-560159-1

1 2 3 4 5 6 7 8 9 10   W   7 6 5 4 3 2 1 0 9 8
Printed and bound in Canada

This book has been meticulously researched and compiled using the latest information
available from Revenue Canada and the Department of Finance at the time of writing.
Because tax and filing procedures are continually changing the author and publisher
cannot be responsible for errors or omissions. We welcome any information that enables
us to clarify or expand on issues of interest to our readers.

This book is sold with the understanding that neither the author nor the publisher is
hereby rendering legal, accounting, or other professional advice. If such advice or other
assistance is required, the personal services of a competent professional should be sought.

Canadian Cataloguing in Publication Data
Jacks, Evelyn, 1955-
 201 easy ways to reduce your taxes

Annual
1996 ed.
ISBN 1204-556X
ISBN 0-07-560159-1 (1998)

1. Income tax – Law and legislation – Canada – Popular works. 2. Tax planning –
Canada – Popular works. I. Title: Reduce your taxes.

HJ4661.A2J33   343.7105'2'05   C96-300293-7

Publisher: Joan Homewood
Editor: Erin Moore
Production Coordinator: Jennifer Burnell
Cover design: Jack Steiner
Editorial services: Rachel Mansfield
Page design/composition: Lynda Powell

To Maureen

Your friendship is a special jewel in my life

ABOUT EVELYN JACKS

Evelyn Jacks is Founder and President of *The Jacks Institute*, a national private career college specializing in tax and business-related courses for individuals and tax industry professionals. She is the author of over 20 best-selling books on personal income tax preparation, and over 70 industry-related training courses. Evelyn is a frequent national commentator on federal and provincial budgets and has criss-crossed Canada for over a dozen years to answer your tax questions on local and national TV and radio programs.

Other books by Evelyn Jacks:

Jacks on Tax Savings: *Everyone's Favourite Canadian Tax Guide to Preparing Income Tax Returns*. 14th edition.

The Complete Canadian Home Business Guide to Taxes.

Jacks on Personal Finance: Modern Money Management for Utterly Confused Canadians. 1st edition.

Jacks on GST: *The Authoritative Guide for Business and Consumers.*

Certificate Courses from The Jacks Institute: These home study courses feature tax software by CANTAX (in French from *L'Impôt Personnel*), and bookkeeping/payroll courses feature software by *Simply Accounting*.

The Quick and Easy Tax Course for Beginners: a simple income tax preparation course for beginners designed to train students to prepare their own income tax returns by computer, or those of friends and family.

The Intermediate Personal Income Tax Preparation Course: a professional entry level course designed to train the student to prepare professional computerized tax returns for others, out of home or office, or gain employment within the financial services industry.

The Computerized Advanced Income Tax Preparation Course: an advanced course for those who wish to prepare tax returns and do tax planning scenarios by computer on a professional basis.

The Computerized Payroll Clerk Course: a skill-oriented course that teaches payroll preparation, T4 Slip preparation, and month end reporting with an emphasis on tax obligations of the employer and employee.

The Small Business Tax Course: for unincorporated business ventures, a detailed course on tax filing provisions including statement preparation, capital acquisitions and dispositions, income and operational deductions.

The Computerized Bookkeeping Course for Small Business: learn how to prepare books by computer for small business enterprises.

The Jacks on Tax Update Newsletter Service: quarterly reports on significant personal tax changes throughout the year.

CONTENTS

INTRODUCTION

Living in the best country in the whole world does not come without its costs. Canadians pay a lot of income taxes. Those considered to be earners, with taxable income of more than $59,180, are in full partnership with the government, which can take up to 50% or more of new dollars earned.

Middle-income earners—those whose taxable income is over $29,590 but under $59,180—pay marginal tax rates of approximately 40% to 44%, depending on their province of residence.

And even low-income earners—those with taxable incomes up to $29,590—pay tax at marginal rates of about 27%. However, in these cases, generous refundable tax credits on both the federal and provincial side of the tax filing equation, have effectively been used to redistribute social benefits to the most needy in our society... provided they file tax returns.

For many, the key financial planning issues, given these tax filing realities, involve security in the future. If you are among those who feel it is time to take control of your taxpaying future, you may wish to ask yourself two key questions:

1. How can I plan the income levels I realize every year to maximize the growth of capital while minimizing taxes and clawbacks, particularly on social benefits such as the Child Tax Benefit, Old Age Security, or Employment Insurance?

2. How can I accumulate enough wealth on an after-tax basis to live well, with or without the public pension system? This question is not only valid but critical in all financial planning activities today, in light of the proposed changes to our current Old Age Security system, which is scheduled to be phased out as soon as the year 2001.

Every dollar you manage to keep in your pockets today, on an after-tax basis, will add to your wealth. Should your personal productivity end or be curtailed, it is this accumulated capital that must produce the dollars you will need to live comfortably in retirement.

It is possible to go about your daily business creating wealth despite the tax laws. We hope to help you do this with simple tax-filing and tax-planning basics described in this book. While the information contained here is not meant to turn you into a tax expert, it is our hope that it will help you ask better questions of your financial advisors, or encourage you to seek more educational opportunities in the interesting field of personal income tax preparation.

THE 10 KEY TAX CHANGES FOR 1997

1. **Most Employees will be subject to an unusual repayment of CPP premiums on the 1997 tax return.** That's because the CPP premium rate was increased in February of 1997, but employers' source deduction tables were likely not. The proper rate of withholding of CPP for 1997 was 3% of maximum contributory earnings; the amount withheld was 2.925%, resulting in a 0.075% shortfall. Revenue Canada will ask you to submit the difference on your 1997 tax return.

2. **Employment Insurance recipients may be jolted when they file their 1997 tax returns**. This is because a new repayment calculation, based on your "claims history" could cost you up to 100% of the EI Benefits you received. If the claims history shows that you have been on regular EI benefits for more than 20 weeks since July of 1996, the base income amount at which the clawback begins will be $39,000. If you have been on EI for less than 20 weeks since July 1996, the net income level allowed before the clawback is invoked is higher—$48,750. On the good news side, those who earned less than $2000 in the year will be entitled to a full refund of their EI premiums.

3. **Recipients of Canada Pension Plan lump sum payments**, including Death Benefits, will be eligible for special tax treatment on the lump sums received after 1995. Revenue Canada will allocate benefits received to the tax year they were payable in, if the amounts exceed $300. Adjust your 1996 tax return if you received amounts that pertained to a prior year.

4. **Capital Gains income may be affected by two unusual circumstances this year.** First, many investors who owned Bre-X shares, or other losers, will want to make capital loss calculations and use them to offset capital gains in 1997 and/or to carry back excess losses to offset gains of the carry-over years. Others will be interested in new rules that give a tax break to those who transfer publicly traded shares to charity.

5. **Separating or divorcing couples will now be affected by new rules**, which render child support paid under agreements negotiated after April 30, 1997, to be non-taxable to the recipient and non-deductible to the payor. Payment under agreements signed prior to May 1, and Spousal Support paid under either scenario, will continue to be taxable to the recipient and tax-deductible to

the payor. These changes will also affect RRSP contribution room of both parties, so planning for now and the future is a good idea.

6. **New auto expense deduction rules** will enable the self-employed or those employees required to use their own car to carry out employment activities, to reap some tax benefits from an enhanced capital cost allowance claim on the acquisition of a "luxury vehicle." A $1000 increase over the previous CCA ceiling level will apply to vehicles, which can now cost up to $25,000 plus PST/GST/HST before restrictions on the write-offs apply. However, if you borrow money to buy your car, the interest expense maximum per month has dropped to $250, while maximum leasing write-offs cannot exceed $550 a month (plus PST/GST/HST).

7. **Students will be happy about the increases in the Education Amount.** $150 a month may be claimed by full-time students at post-secondary schools (or part-time disabled students); an increase over last year's $100 amount. In addition, students may claim certain ancillary fees and charges other than student association fees, as eligible tuition fees. Starting in 1997, a student may also carry forward unused tuition and education credits to future tax years, if this is more advantageous from a tax viewpoint.

8. **Medical expenses are often underclaimed on the tax return**, and starting in 1997 such omissions can hurt twice as much. That's because there is a new Refundable Medical Expense Supplement, available to low-income working families, that is based on the medical expense tax credit you applied for elsewhere on your return. There are several new classes of medical expenses that can be claimed—including 50% of air conditioning costs incurred by those with severe ailments—and up to $10,000 in home care costs.

9. **Charitable taxpayers will get further tax breaks.** Starting in 1997 you can give up to 75% of your net income to charity (100% in the year of death or the immediately preceding year). Further enhancements to this net income limit account for the taxable portion of capital assets given, or recapture on depreciable property.

10. **1997 is the final tax year in which Forward Averaging Tax Credits can be claimed**. If you previously forward averaged income, and now are at a lower tax bracket, you may have some money coming back to you, simply by completing Form T581. Such forward averaging would have appeared on your returns in the years prior to 1988, so it might be worthwhile to check back.

TAX PLANNING REALLY PAYS OFF

Do you know...

* *You should file a tax return even if you don't have taxable income...*
* *You should prepare family tax returns starting with the lowest-income earner...*
* *There are ways to transfer income from higher earner to lower earner...*
* *Life insurance policy proceeds can be received tax free...*

The objective of tax planning is to legally minimize the amount of tax you pay by arranging your affairs within the framework of the law so that you'll pay the least amount possible. This is your right and duty as a Canadian taxpayer.

Effective tax planning involves a multi-year approach to your tax-filing routine. The best way to begin on your journey toward tax savings is to assess your family's current income situation, tax-filing routine and spending habits, now, and to commit to planning to pay only the correct amount of taxes necessary. To make this committment, you'll need to know more about the rate of tax you are currently paying, how to legally split income within the family, how to diversify income to take advantage of different marginal tax rates, and how to consolidate your relationship with Revenue Canada to make sure you are the one in control of your after-tax dollars.

Almost every Canadian can benefit from a little tax knowledge. In Canada, we have a tax system that does more than collect taxes from the masses: it also redistributes income to the poor and the working poor. Even if you have little or no income, if you are over the age of 18 you should be filing a tax return to take advantage of a series of refundable tax credits, available through both the federal and certain provincial governments.

For some, the tax return is an application for new monthly income, or the source of tax savings against future income. For these reasons, filing an income tax return can be the most important financial transaction of the year.

Average Canadians look upon tax season with dread, unfortunately. For example, June, a part-time teacher, and Sam, a self-employed architect, are concerned about the amount of tax they are paying in light of the rapidly approaching prospect of financing this year's cost of braces ($3,000) for their daughter, Maggie, and university expenses ($5,000) for their son, Jason. There were never any savings opportunities in the choices the family had made in the past.

With no salary bonuses or business income increases in sight, the family must now find a way to make $8,000 of new, after-tax dollars appear, and soon! Wisely, they turn to their tax return for help. To their surprise, they find that by spending a little time in getting to know tax provisions that apply to them, they can save money.

There are twelve simple "starter" tax tips every family should follow every year:

1 ALWAYS FILE A TAX RETURN

Even if you do not have a taxable income, it pays to file a tax return. Lower-income earners who wish to receive refundable benefits, such as the Child Tax Benefit (CTB), the Goods and Services Tax Credit Prepayment (GSTC), or the new Refundable Medical Expense Supplement, must file a tax return, as do residents of certain provinces that feature refundable tax credits.

Seniors who do not file income tax returns may not receive the right amount of Old Age Security. And investors may miss out on carrying forward important information such as RRSP Room, or capital loss balances. Others may miss carrying over unused deductions such as moving expenses, home office expenses, employment or business losses.

Remind any dependant you have who turned 19 during the year to file for his or her own GST Credit, or in some provinces, refundable provincial tax credits. Payments in the calendar year received for January through June will be based on income figures on the prior year, while July to December payments will be based on information recorded on the current return. This credit is worth close to $200 (or more in the case of working singles), so it's well worth the tax-filing time.

2 ALWAYS PREPARE FAMILY TAX RETURNS TOGETHER

Tax filing should be a coordinated family event. To maximize your tax savings as a family unit, prepare family tax returns at the same time, starting with the lowest-income earner and finishing with the higher earner. You now have the required net and taxable income figures to maximize provisions such as the Spousal Amount, as well as transferable provisions such as the Age Amount, the $1,000 Pension Income Amount, the Tuition and Education Credits for full-time students and disabled dependents, medical expenses and RRSP transfers. You might even qualify as a family for refundable tax credits under both federal and provincial rules, including the new Manitoba Learning Tax Credit, the new B.C. Family Bonus, and the new Alberta Employment Tax Credits.

3 REVIEW PRIOR-FILED TAX RETURNS

Always have a copy of tax returns for the immediate prior tax year on hand. This will allow you to preview any changes in your "taxpayer profile" by making a list of personal or financial circumstances that have occurred during the most recent tax year. You will also be prompted to send for auxiliary tax forms from Revenue Canada, or to move from a "short form" such as the T1 Special to the T1 General Return should you have a more complicated tax situation this year.

You will also be alerted to any missed tax provisions. These can be recovered in most circumstances for each tax year as far back as 1985, simply by requesting an adjustment to your prior-filed returns. Revenue Canada provides a special form for this purpose, called a T1ADJ.

4   CREATE RRSP ROOM

Earnings from employment or self-employment, net rental income, and even certain maintenance or alimony payments made under agreements in place before May 1, 1997, will qualify as "earned income" for RRSP purposes.

Contributing to the RRSP may have little benefit this year if you are not taxable. However, you may carry forward any undeducted contributions for use in the future. As well, RRSP contribution "room" can be carried forward *on an indefinite basis* to future tax years when income may be higher. Therefore, filing a tax return — even when you have a small income — may create a "future tax deduction" to offset income at that time. That can save you big dollars!

5   ALWAYS FILE ON TIME

Tardiness is expensive, especially if your return is filed late on purpose. It never makes sense to let Revenue Canada hang on to your tax refund. Further, if you filed late, thinking that you were owed a refund, but Revenue Canada later reassesses you and creates a balance due, interest and late filing penalties will be charged back to the original tax year.

By filing on time, midnight April 30 for most people, you can avoid a late filing penalty of 5% of the outstanding taxes due plus 1% per month of the outstanding balance for a maximum of 12 months. In addition, Revenue Canada will charge you interest on balances outstanding at what is known as the "prescribed rate" — the rate paid on treasury bills for the last quarter **plus** 4%. This can become very expensive.

Unincorporated small business owners and their spouses have until June 15 to file, but interest on any balance due is charged back to April 30. If Revenue Canada owes you a tax refund, no interest is paid to you until the return is filed and then only 45 days after the later of (1) the date the return is filed, or (2) the date the return was required to be file.

Note: In the 1996 tax filing year, June 15 fell on a Sunday. Taxpayers were given until Monday, June 16 to file their unincorporated small business returns. However, in some regions Revenue Canada's computer system was mistakenly set on the June 15 date. This caused a late filing penalty to be generated on the returns filed June 16 with a balance due. If this happened to you, be sure to request an adjustment to remove the late filing penalty.

6 KNOW WHO MUST FILE

You are required to file a tax return if you owe the government money for the tax year; or if you disposed of a capital property, such as a cottage or mutual fund. You must file if you are wishing to receive Old Age Security pension in the future or if Canada Pension Plan contributions are required on your self-employment profits. Revenue Canada may send you a formal request to file, in which case you must file a tax return.

You will want to file to claim refunds owed to you or to file for refundable tax credits, such as the Goods and Services Tax Credit, or certain carry-over provisions. Filing on time can also create handsome monthly "returns" for your family. For example, both spouses must file a tax return in order to receive the monthly Child Tax Benefit for children under the age of 19.

7 DECLARE YOUR FOREIGN ASSETS

You can avoid some hefty penalties in the future if you are aware that for tax years 1996 and 1997 you will be required to report transfers and loans to a foreign trust, distributions from a foreign trust and any interests in foreign trusts with the 1997 return. The requirement to report foreign investment properties worth more than $100,000 has been postponed to April of 1999 pending a review of the proposals. The revision was to have included funds or tangible property in foreign bank accounts, securities held outside Canada and shares of Canadian companies deposited with a foreign broker. The reporting of holdings in IRAs (Individual Retirement Accounts), shares in a non-resident corporation, interest in certain non-resident trusts, intangible property, and tangible property, such as commercial real estate, would also be caught. Specifically excluded from the proposed disclosure requirements is information about property used exclusively in an active business, personal use property (such as cottages, cars and boats), and property in an RRSP, RRIF, and a registered pension plan.

A special reporting form is also available for disclosure of foreign affiliates (T1134), transfers or loans to a foreign trust (T1141), and distributions from foreign trusts (T1142). There are three types of exempt trusts: (1) a foreign retirement arrangement, (2) a trust establishing employee benefits under superannuation or retirement funds, or a

...t least 150 beneficiaries of the same
value requirements.

...ated that those who fail to disclose their
...s subject to penalties of $500 a month for the
...aximum of $12,000. After this an additional
...be levied.

...HE T1 GENERAL TAX FORM

Despite ...evenue Canada's attempts to simplify the tax return, Canadians who really want to be sure they are claiming every tax deduction and credit they are entitled to should use the T1 General Tax Form. This is the only tax form that makes reference to all the tax deductions, tax credits and tax calculations to which you are entitled. Knowledge about this form also makes the transition to computer tax software use easier.

9 GET THE FAMILY INVOLVED IN TAX-WISE SAVINGS

One of the best ways to minimize the tax you pay is to try to transfer income from the higher-income earner to the lower earners in the family. This is called "income splitting." However, one must be very careful not to invoke the "Attribution Rules."

The Attribution Rules ensure that when certain assets are transferred from a high-earning spouse to the lower-earning spouse or child, resulting income is taxed back to the high-income earner. If, for example, you transfer interest-bearing investments, such as a Canada Savings Bond, to your spouse, or a child who is under 18 years of age, the resulting earnings will be taxed back to you. But there are ways to legally circumvent these Attribution Rules. These are discussed at length in Chapter 3.

10 FORCE YOURSELF TO INVEST YOUR TAX SAVINGS

For many taxpayers, the income tax refund is one of the largest capital receipts of the year.

Through electronic filing capabilities, you can have the money deposited directly into your bank account, under the general principle that "What can't be seen can't be spent!" Then, invest your tax refund wisely. A portion of the new funds could also be used to pay down your mortgage, credit card balances or other debts whose interest charges are non-deductible. The rest of the funds could be used to create new money; that is, by topping up your RRSP first, if you qualify to make contributions, and then other "non-registered" investments.

It's possible Grandma really had something in that saying, "A penny saved is a penny earned."

11 RETHINK YOUR SPENDING DECISIONS

One of the main reasons that taxpayers miss claiming tax deductions or credits is a lack of appreciation of the benefits a tax viewpoint can have on decision making. The wise tax planner won't make any personal or financial decision without considering all tax-planning alternatives first.

Sam, our architect, is in the market for a new car. He wants a Mercedes. He can afford a moped.

With his dream in the background, he contemplates an important decision: Do I buy a new or used car? First, he considers the tax implications of leasing or buying the vehicle. (See Chapter 5 for more details.) Then, he steps outside this mindset to assess carefully the alternative uses for his money.

After much deliberation, Sam buys a used Ford.

He then takes the difference in savings between the new and used car costs and splits them in two ways: one-third of the money is salted away in an investment fund for safekeeping to be used for future repairs, as the used car has no warranty. The earnings on this investment also finance the annual licence and insurance fees.

Two-thirds of the savings are invested in Sam's RRSP, which at his marginal tax rate reaps a tax saving of 48% of his investment, which he receives in just three weeks after electronically filing his tax return. These savings are invested in another fund that Sam nicknames "The Mercedes Fund." Every year his tax savings from the RRSP investment add to the fund, which can be used to finance a downpayment for the car.

Sam soon finds the need to reassess his options in light of the rapidly accumulating Mercedes Fund. Does he really want the luxury car, or is there a better investment-oriented decision he can make?

Funny thing about money — it's always either in your pocket, or someone else's. Used as a tool to create wealth, Sam will get better mileage from his after-tax dollar.

New in '97 12 SPREAD THE WEALTH WITHIN THE FAMILY

In most families, the higher-income earner typically invests money, and the lower earner spends part-time earnings or social benefit payments, such as tax refunds or the Goods and Services Tax Credit, on consumer goods.

Consider, for a moment, the benefit of the opposite strategy: if the lower-income earner invested social benefit payments or other income sources received, the investment earnings on those principal amounts would be included in that person's income.

The result: more of the investment income would stay in the family because it would be taxed at a lower tax rate, if at all.

It makes sense to use a tax focus when making decisions about your money. For example, use the monies earned by the higher earner to maximize an RRSP investment, as this will reap progressively higher tax benefits the higher your tax bracket.

RRSP deposit decisions can also lead to tax-wise income-splitting. By making the RRSP contribution in the name of the lower-earning spouse, subsequent withdrawals in retirement will be taxed at the lower earner's tax rate, provided certain holding requirements are met.

Lower earners who are taxable should also consider making an RRSP contribution, if they have RRSP "room." The resulting lower net income might create higher Child Tax Benefit or GST Credit returns, a higher new Refundable Medical Expense Supplement, or additional deductions or credits for the higher-income earner.

Wealth creation and wealth preservation can be multiplied if you involve every family member.

chapter 2

STARTING OFF RIGHT

Do you know...

* *Filing an accurate tax return is the first step in reaping tax savings...*
* *Planning a move to another province can bring you a tax refund windfall...*
* *Most taxpayers don't know the lucrative tax deductions they are entitled to...*
* *Deductions missed in previous years can be easily recovered...*

Someone once said that nothing is too difficult if you break it down into parts. That principle certainly holds true when it comes to income tax preparation. Most people know and understand that they must file a tax return every year, or face financial consequences. However, tax filing time is no time to plan to reduce the level of your tax bill. . . when you file this year's return, you're basically recording history. To minimize your lifetime tax bill, it is the planning you do throughout the year that will reap for you the kind of tax savings you might think your neighbours are getting. What do they know that you don't?

There are a few basic parameters that every taxpayer should know about the taxes they pay. These can be summarized as follows:

1. Understand the rate of tax you pay on your income sources.
2. Create wealth by minimizing taxes on the income you and your investments produce.

3. Preserve wealth by sheltering your capital with tax deferrals and income splitting.

4. Listen for and understand the annual changes to your tax return.

So let's begin the process of tax saving with the step we all know the best: the filing of an income tax return.

13 KNOW HOW TO DO IT YOURSELF IN SIX EASY STEPS

There are several key figures on the tax return that will affect the amount of tax you pay and whether you qualify for a refundable tax credit from provincial and/or the federal government. Every taxpayer should know about the six basic steps of the tax-filing routine and how to identify them on the T1 General Tax Return, even if you use computer software to prepare your return:

Step 1 Identification and Goods and Services Tax Credit Application

Step 2 Total Income Calculation (Up to Line 150)

Step 3 Net Income Calculation (Up to Line 236)

Step 4 Taxable Income Calculation (Includes Line 236-Net Income-and finishes at Line 260)

Step 5 Non-Refundable Tax Credits (Up to Line 350)

Step 6 Refund or Balance Owing (Finishes at either Line 484 or Line 485)

One of the most important lines is the calculation of Net Income (line 236 of the tax return). That is the figure upon which credits like the Goods and Services Tax Credit, the Child Tax Benefit, the new Refundable Medical Expense Supplement and provincial tax credits are based.

14 FILE IN THE CORRECT PROVINCE OF RESIDENCE

Where were you on New Year's Eve? In Canada we file one tax return to compute federal taxes, and that same tax return is used to compute the provincial portion of taxes in all provinces except Quebec. (There, a separate provincial return is required.) You are taxed at the provincial tax rate of your province of residence as of December 31 of the tax year, and this is usually a percentage of basic federal tax. So, if a move is in your future, try to time it with a tax-wise eye. That is, move to a province with lower tax rates before year end, so that your entire year's income is taxed at this lower rate. If you are going to a province with a higher tax rate, try to move early in the new year to ensure adequate source deductions will be made.

New in '97 15 KNOW HOW TO ARRIVE AT NET INCOME TO INCREASE TAX CREDITS

You know that Net Income — Line 236 — influences the size of your Refundable Tax Credits. Net income is also the figure that is used in calculating numerous other tax provisions, including the amount of Old Age Security Pension received, the amount of repayment, if any, required by Employment Insurance recipients, the Spousal Amount, the Equivalent-to-Spouse Amount, the claim for Additional Personal Amounts, medical expenses, and charitable donations. This figure is also used to compute certain provincial tax credits, some of which may be refundable, and provincial net income taxes.

By reducing your net income, you may receive more under each of these other tax provisions which, in the case of the Child Tax Benefit, can affect your monthly cash flow. You'll also reduce any provincial net income taxes you may be subject to. (In the case of donations, a lower net income may restrict your claims.)

If you do nothing else, make sure you maximize the specific deductions available to reduce income in your individual circumstances. Lower earners who are taxable should also consider making an RRSP contribution, if they have RRSP "room." The resulting lower net income might create higher new Refundable Medical Expense Supplement, Child Tax Benefit, GST Credits, or other deductions or credits for the higher-income earner.

New in '97 16 IDENTIFY TAX SAVERS THAT WILL REDUCE YOUR NET INCOME

Which of the following tax deductions have you missed taking advantage of over the past several years?
- Registered Pension Plan Contributions
- RRSP Contributions
- Union/Professional Dues (Did you claim a GST/HST* Rebate for any GST/HST charged on dues?)
- Child Care Expenses

---

* The HST came into effect in certain provinces on April 1, 1997.

- Attendant Care Expenses
- Business Investment Losses
- Moving Expenses
- Alimony or Separation Allowance paid in the year of separation or the immediately prior year, based on agreements in place before May 1, 1997 or in all cases, Spousal Support paid
- Carrying Charges, such as Safety Deposit Box Fees, and interest on non-registered investments
- Exploration and Development Expenses
- Other Employment Expenses, such as auto expenses or home office costs
- Repayments of social benefits such as Employment Insurance Benefits.

P.S. Some less obvious deductions include the $500 exemption on scholarship or bursary income for students. Only the net amount, after the exemption, must be reported in income. So be sure to read the fine print for every line on the tax return.

17 REDUCE TAXABLE INCOME WITH CREATIVE DEDUCTIONS

Another group of deductions available on the tax return are rather obscure but can be lucrative. This is the specialized set of deductions used to arrive at taxable income, which is the figure on which federal tax is calculated. Check to see if you qualify to claim the following for the current or prior tax years:

- Employee Home Relocation Loan Deduction
- Stock Option and Shares Deduction
- Other Payments Deduction (for Workers' Compensation, Social Assistance or Federal Old Age Supplements added to income for the current tax year)
- Deduction for Non-Taxable Receipts of Foreign Pensions (such as German Pensions)
- Losses of Prior Years from Limited Partnerships; Non-Capital Losses; Capital Losses since 1972
- Capital Gains Deduction
- Northern Residents' Deduction
- Deduction for Child Support received from a U.S. resident or other income tax exempt by virtue of a foreign tax treaty.

18 DEFER INCOME TO FUTURE YEARS

Individual taxpayers must report most income on a cash basis; that is, when received in the calendar year, January to December. Generally, when you transfer income from a year of high earnings to a year of lower earnings you will reap tax rewards.

Mike and Maureen, for example, own a duplex that they use as a rental property. In order to meet their financial commitments, they are considering selling it. They know that 75% of their expected profit of $35,000 each will be added to their income in the year of sale. With proper planning, timing, and the presence of a willing purchaser, this couple may be able to cut down their tax liability by selling one half of the duplex late this year and the other half early next year.

In another example, Meg and Matthew are expecting their first child in the spring. Meg will be staying home from work until the end of that tax year, after the baby is born. This might be a good tax year in which to realize capital gains income from the sale of an asset, or to make an RRSP withdrawal, as the income would be taxed at a lower marginal rate.

The idea is to keep as much of the income as possible in the lowest tax bracket. This can be accomplished in some cases by reporting the income over two tax years, or by deferring the reporting of other income to a year of lower earnings.

19 PRESERVE DEDUCTIONS LIKE THE RRSP

You may wish, at your discretion, to defer certain tax deductions for use in future years when your income is higher than it might be today. Planning to save RRSP room is a good example. Taxpayers can carry forward unused contribution room in their RRSP account. If you were eligible to contribute $5,000 in each of the years 1991 to 1996 for a total of $30,000, but could only afford to contribute $1,000 each year, you would have $24,000 in unused contribution room to carry forward and use on the 1997 return. The contribution must actually be made to be deductible, either during the year or in the first 60 days of the new year. Starting in 1996, RRSP room can be carried forward indefinitely.

By planning wisely, you can use that room to offset a year of high income — perhaps when you dispose of a capital property, or receive a bonus. That's the time the unused RRSP contribution room of prior years can be used to reduce significantly — or even eliminate — the amount of tax that is payable on these unusual transactions.

20 LEARN TO PLAY THE GAME WITH REVENUE CANADA

Someone once said that the relationship a taxpayer has with Revenue Canada is not unlike that of two teams in a football game. Both are trying to control the football and score points. There are, however, a couple of real differences in playing ball with Revenue Canada.

First, instead of a football, you are playing with your own money. This can put an entirely different "spin" on your positioning. Second, you are playing a game with an opponent who is also the referee and knows all of the rules, plus a few others that are not published information. You may work very hard, but without an even playing field your odds of getting that football — your money — into the end zone (that is, into your own pocket) are not that good...unless, of course, you too know the rules.

The moral of this tip? Make an effort to keep up with basic tax changes every year. It will pay off over the long run. Or, if tax training camp doesn't suit you, hire some talent to help you score some financial touchdowns.

21 RECAPTURE PREVIOUSLY OVERPAID TAXES

Taxpayers can now request an adjustment to a prior-filed tax return, or recover tax refunds for missed returns of prior years, all the way back to 1985. This is a great way to recover new disposable income, when you're in a cash flow pinch.

If you forgot to claim your annual safety deposit box fee of $65 a year, over a ten-year period, for example, you will have missed $650 worth of legitimate tax deductions. This translates into $273 in overpaid taxes at a 42% marginal tax rate, or $27.30 each year. All it takes is a letter to the tax department to recoup your losses.

If you didn't file a return in the past and you suspect you may have money coming back from refundable tax credits or overpaid source deductions, file the tax return(s) in question now. Revenue Canada won't send a refund to you unless you ask for it.

22 RECOVER THE OLD FEDERAL SALES TAX CREDIT

In 1991, the Federal Sales Tax Credit was discontinued. However, it is important to note that taxpayers may file to recover missed credits. At risk of missing out were those who turned 19 in the year or low-income seniors. A summary of refundable credits and income thresholds follows:

Federal Sales Tax Credit	1986	1987	1988	1989	1990
Per Adult	$50	$50	$70	$100	$140
Per Child	$25	$25	$35	$50	$70
Net Income Threshold	$15,000	$15,000	$16,000	$16,000	$18,000

If this happened to you write a letter to Revenue Canada requesting the Federal Sales Tax Credit to be sent to you for each year in which you were eligible.

23 REQUEST THAT INTEREST AND PENALTIES BE WAIVED IN SEVERE HARDSHIP CASES

If circumstances beyond your control — a serious accident or illness, serious emotional or mental distress, including a death in the family, or a natural or man-made disaster — caused you to miss making a tax payment when due, Revenue Canada can waive the penalty and interest charges that would otherwise be imposed under the law for failure to file or to pay.

The same new rule applies if the penalties or interest resulted from erroneous actions at the tax department, such as processing delays that caused you not to be informed in a reasonable time period of an amount that was owing, errors in written matters, incorrect advice on instalment remittance billings, or errors in processing the information on your return.

You can request that interest and penalties be cancelled or waived in such cases by making a written submission to the tax department, outlining the facts and reasons for your position that the events were out of your control.

This tip can save you thousands of dollars, if Revenue Canada agrees with your position.

24 FLOOD DISASTER VICTIMS CAN FIND TAX RELIEF

A good example of the exceptions that Revenue Canada will make to accommodate hardship cases occurred in the 1997 tax year in Manitoba. Victims of the Flood of the Century will find tax relief on their 1997 tax returns in cases where the flooding caused late filing, or where employers provided financial assistance.

Financial assistance given by an employer to employees will not be taxed as a benefit if certain conditions are met:

- the assistance was reasonable under the circumstances
- the assistance was based on an employer–employee relationship and not because the employee holds shares in the business
- the employer must have granted the assistance on a voluntary basis
- the employer must have made the payment without regard for the employee's work performance, length of service or any other work-related factor
- the employer cannot have granted financial assistance in exchange for past or future services
- the employer cannot have used the financial assistance given to compensate the employee for the loss of employment income.

Employers were not required to withhold taxes on these payments and will be allowed to deduct these payments as business expenses. A list of the names, addresses and social insurance numbers of the employees so paid must be sent to the Winnipeg Tax Services Office at 325 Broadway, R3C 4T4 with an explanatory note. Employees will not be required to report these payments on their tax returns, and no computation for CPP/EI premiums is required. The amounts will not increase earned income for RRSP purposes.

25 MINIMIZE EXPOSURE TO REVENUE CANADA CHARGES

You already know that by filing on time, midnight April 30, you can avoid a late filing penalty of 5% of the outstanding taxes due plus 1% per month of the outstanding balance for a maximum of 12 months. The filing deadline has been extended to June 15 for unincorporated small businesses, but an interest charge still applies from May 1 on if you owe money to Revenue Canada.

Interest charges can also be avoided on balances resulting from deficient quarterly instalments, or gross negligence penalties which, by the way, can be avoided entirely if you tell Revenue Canada about under-reported income or overstated expenses before they find out. Voluntary compliance can reduce your tax audit costs significantly. So, if you have a guilty conscience, request an adjustment to prior-filed returns to correct any erroneous filing. It can pay off handsomely to have a spotless filing record with Revenue Canada.

26 KEEP YOUR WELL-ORGANIZED TAX RECORDS FOR AT LEAST SIX YEARS

Probably the most difficult part of filing a tax return is gathering all the information to outline the past year of your life. All most employees must do is wait for their T4 slips to arrive; others look to their mailbox for T5s (investment income summaries) or various pension income amounts.

If you are self-employed, a commission salesperson or an investor, some transactions are self-reported. The onus of proof for all figures on the tax return rests with you. Always file a return with one thought in mind: Will these documents and figures pass a tax audit?

The answer to that question depends largely on how well you'll remember the justification for your claims two or three years from now when the auditor may call on you. Keep meticulous notes in your working papers.

Keep logs and journals of your business travels or the number of clients you see in your home office. When you entertain, write the name of your client or associate on the back of the chit, as well as the purpose of the meeting. Keep your records for a minimum of six years from the end of the calendar year in which you received your Notice of Assessment.

27 USE CARRY-OVER OPPORTUNITIES

You can take certain unused tax deductions or credits incurred in one year and use them to offset income or taxes in another year. This can mean recovery of prior-paid taxes or the reduction of future tax liabilities. Check your old tax returns for the following provisions:

1. *Home office expenses:* these cannot be used to increase or create a loss from employment or self-employment. Unused claims can be carried forward and applied next year.

2. *Unused donations* can be carried forward for a five-year period. (This year you can claim up to 75% of net income, so this could be lucrative.)

3. *Moving expenses* can be carried forward if expenses exceed income earned at the new location.

4. *An accumulated forward averaging amount* at the end of 1996 can be applied for the last time to the 1997 tax return. (This provision will end in 1997.)

5. *An Alternative Minimum Tax Amount* paid in a prior year may be used to reduce taxes this year.

6. *A Capital Cost Allowance Claim* for those with small businesses, farms or rental properties may be claimed to the taxpayer's advantage.

Other important information to be carried forward:

7. Unused non-capital losses of prior years.

8. Unused capital losses of prior years.

9. Unused Capital Gains Deduction room of prior years for the purposes of the $500,000 Super Exemption still available to owners of Small Business Corporation Shares or Qualifying Farm Properties. (Use Form T657 to make this claim.)

10. Cumulative Net Investment Losses.

11. Unused RRSP contribution room.

12. Paid and unclaimed periodic maintenance payments for up to one year before a formal agreement was finalized.

13. Unused Business Investment Losses.

14. The amount of your Capital Gains Election and the new Adjusted Cost Base of your assets, including the exempt gains balances available for mutual funds or eligible capital property on which an election was made.

15. Fair Market Value (FMV) of assets acquired by gift, transfer or inheritance.

16. Any unused amounts of a student's tuition/education tax credits.

Upon request, Revenue Canada can also update you on their records of your capital and non-capital loss balances, or unclaimed home office expenses. To be sure, however, it is best to keep these records on statements filed with your personal tax records, and to review last year's carry-over balances.

Also, be sure to instruct the executor of your estate or other trusted assistants about these carry-over balances, so they have the information should you become incapacitated. Because such events are normally unforeseen, a highly organized tax portfolio will make life easier for those who act on your behalf, and could save you and your family thousands of dollars.

28 BREAK THE TASK DOWN

Start early in the year to prepare your family's taxes, and then use a three-step process to finish the task.

Step one: gather and separate all information about each family member, including birthdates, Social Insurance Numbers, and source documents for income and deductions. Make sure you have a tax return and the appropriate tax guide for each provision. Separate the T-slips and sort copies for submission to Revenue Canada. Obtain any auxiliary tax forms for deductions such as child care expenses from the government before you start to compute your taxes.

Step two is to enter the data and begin the number crunching.

Step three, which should be done after a break away from this work, is the checking and assembly of the tax return for mailing or electronic filing.

If you have recently acquired a computer, you may also wish to try preparing your taxes using one of the many excellent software packages available. This is a great way to take control of the amount of tax you pay, and to do some tax planning throughout the year.

CHAPTER 3

PLANNING A FAMILY INCLUDES TAX SAVINGS

Do you know...

* *The tax system offers a monthly income to certain families with children...*
* *There are ample opportunities to reduce tax by splitting income within the family...*
* *Maximizing your available tax deductions can reduce your net income...*
* *Lower net family incomes can reap higher federal and provincial credits...*
* *Every Canadian can earn up to $6,456 tax free...*

Tax assistance for those who live with a family comes in a variety of formats in Canada. The taxpayer may claim deductions that reduce taxable income, non-refundable tax credits that are used to reduce the actual taxes paid, and tax-free refundable tax credits that are sent to certain Canadians, whose incomes fall under certain pre-set thresholds.

The most lucrative of these provisions is the tax-free Child Tax Benefit. Every three months Revenue Canada distributes approximately $450 million dollars in Child Tax Benefits to over three million families across Canada. The CTB can only be received if a tax return is filed by both parents of a child, because the amount received is based on net family income.

To reduce your net income, the next step in the chain of provisions available to families includes the claiming of child care expenses and

RRSP deductions, as well as child support payments for certain taxpayers who signed agreements with their ex-spouses before May 1, 1997.

Finally, it is important to work with the available non-refundable tax credits for the Basic Personal Amount, the Spousal or Equivalent-to-Spouse Amounts, Amounts for Infirm Dependents, Disability Amounts, tuition and education amounts, medical expenses, and charitable donations.

The key to maximizing your tax-free benefits from the government is to use all applicable tax deductions to reduce your net income and your taxes payable. Next, claim all the Non-Refundable Tax Credits you are entitled to. Then, transferrable tax deductions and credits can be used to reduce the tax liability of supporting persons.

In addition it is important to do some basic investment planning, to use every opportunity to have lower-income earners generate the investment earnings both inside and outside an RRSP. To do so, however, it is necessary to know how to avoid Revenue Canada's Attribution Rules. (See Tips 38 to 48.)

By filing tax returns as a unit, rather than as individuals, it is possible to reduce the family tax burden. Start with the lowest-income earner and work your way up.

29 KNOW THE NEW DEFINITION OF A SPOUSE

For tax purposes, your spouse can be someone of the opposite sex to whom you are legally married, in which case you may be able to claim for the Spousal Amount of up to $5380.

If you are living in a common-law relationship with someone of the opposite sex, that person will be considered your spouse for income tax purposes if you lived together in one of two circumstances. First, if you lived together on December 31 and that person is the parent of your child (naturally or adoptive), you are considered spouses for tax purposes, regardless of how long you've lived together. Second, if you don't have a child together, the spousal status exists if you have lived with that person in a conjugal relationship for a period of 12 months ending in the tax year, or for a continuous 12-month period sometime in the past. When this 12-month period is calculated, include any period of separation less than 90 days.

If you meet these qualifications, you can claim your common-law spouse for the "Spousal Amount" and take advantage of all other transferable provisions available to married couples through the tax system.

✦30 COMMON-LAW UNIONS CAN CHANGE YOUR TAX PICTURE

Over a year ago, Jody and Mark decided to move in together. Previously, each of them had filed their own tax returns as single individuals, to recover overpaid taxes through their employer, and to file for the GST Credit and their provincial refundable tax credits.

This year, their tax-filing profile has changed. If Jody has no income, Mark could make a full claim for her under a non-refundable tax credit called the "Spousal Amount," even though they are not married. If she did have income, the Spousal Amount might be reduced or eliminated. They may also qualify for the new Refundable Medical Expense Supplement if they combine medical receipts (see Tip 204).

However, their new living arrangements would reduce or eliminate their GST Credit and certain provincial tax credits. This is because these claims would now be based on their combined net family income.

31 IN LOVE AND IN WAR, TIMING CAN MAKE THE DIFFERENCE

In the year of marriage, the spouse's net income for the whole year is used for the purposes of determining tax credits and deductions. If the net income of your new spouse is low now, and if that spouse expects to earn more next year, consider planning the marriage before the end of the current tax year to create a Spousal Amount on your tax return sooner. The tax savings might finance at least a part of the honeymoon!

On the other hand, there may be tax advantages to postponing the wedding where there are children in the family unit who are not the product of a union with your spouse-to-be. In that case, you'll be considered single if you and your common-law spouse have not lived together for at least one year in the current year or sometime in the past. This means that you can preserve an Equivalent-to-Spouse Amount for your child at least for this tax year.

Because the size of the Spousal Amount you can claim is dependent upon your spouse's net income, you should be able to reduce net income size with certain allowable tax deductions such as the RRSP or the Child Care Expense deduction.

32 CLAIM THE EQUIVALENT-TO-SPOUSE AMOUNT IF YOU'RE A SINGLE PARENT

A single person, or someone who is divorced, separated or widowed will qualify to claim the Equivalent-to-Spouse Amount for a dependent child who is under 18 and with whom s/he lived during the year. The claim is also extended to those singles who supported a dependent parent or grandparent, or a relative over 18 who is mentally or physically infirm.

The claim is lucrative; it is calculated the same way as the Spousal Amount. That means that if the dependant had a net income of less than $538, the full claim of $5,380 is allowed. That calculates out to an actual federal-provincial tax saving of about $1,500, depending on your provincial tax rate. There are more savings, through an enhanced GST Credit and various provincial tax provisions, aimed at recognizing the dependant's Equivalent-to-Spouse status.

For unmarried parents of the same child who live together in a common law relationship, the Equivalent-to-Spouse Amount for the child is denied. Possible tax relief can be obtained by claiming the Spousal Amount elsewhere in the tax return for the common-law spouse, depending on that person's net income.

If you and your spouse were separated but then reconciled during the year, you can choose to claim the Spousal Amount or the Equivalent-to-Spouse. This is a new provision in 1997.

33 BOTH SPOUSES MUST FILE TO RECEIVE THE MONTHLY CHILD TAX BENEFIT

You can stop looking. There are a number of provisions relating to the expenses of raising a child on the tax form, but there is no place to actually "claim" a separate amount for a dependant under the age of 19. You will want to apply for the Child Tax Benefit, though. All you need to know is that this is done automatically, simply by filing a tax return...no special forms are needed at all.

So, the worst mistake you can make if you are a low- to middle-income earner with children is to commit FTF (Failure to File). The Child Tax Benefit, which is a lucrative monthly payment to Canadian families, can only be received if *both spouses* file a tax return every year.

The Child Tax Benefit payment for your children is therefore determined through the size of the "family net income." The parent and the qualified dependent must reside together in the same home in Canada; therefore non-resident dependents will not qualify.

If the child resides with two parents in two different locations concurrently, only one parent can be eligible in any given month to receive the benefits. In that case, the primary caregiver must be identified. This is determined by specifics on who gives the most details of care. The person who is "eligible" — that is, qualified by the net family income as per the income tax return — receives the Child Tax Benefit.

If the child leaves one parent's home to live with another, the second parent becomes eligible for the credit in the month the dependent starts living with him/her. If the dependent leaves the home for a temporary absence (i.e., holiday, school, work, medical care), the parent still qualifies to receive the benefits throughout the child's temporary period of absence.

The Child Tax Benefit will not be computed at all if neither parent files a tax return. Or, where only one person files, the Child Tax Benefit will be advanced to you for a while, "with warnings." Then repayment is demanded should your spouse fail to file — another compelling reason to invest, rather than spend, this particular government cheque!

34 THE NEWLY ENHANCED WORKING SUPPLEMENT FOR PARENTS

Revenue Canada calculates the CTB based on the number of children under 19 entered on the tax return, the family net income, the family "working income," and the child care expense deductions claimed. There is a basic benefit of $1,020* ($85 a month) for each child under age 19; a supplement of $75 ($6.25 a month) for the third and each additional child; and a further supplement of $213 ($17.75 a month) for each child under age seven. (However, this latter amount is reduced by 25% of any child care amount claimed on the tax return.)

There's more: the Family Working Supplement for low-income earners provides for an additional per-child amount to low-income families. This amounts to $605 for the first child, $405 for the second and $330 for the third and subsequent children. Reductions in the supplement will apply at certain income levels. (See later Tax Tips.)

"Working income" is defined as income from employment, self-employment, training allowances or scholarships, and disability payments under the Canada Pension Plan. (Capital gains resulting from

---

* Note: The figures will change in Alberta and Quebec. In April 1996 B.C. introduced the B.C. Family Bonus. Also, starting in July 1997 Revenue Canada will administer the Alberta Family Employment Tax Credit.

foreclosures or repossessions under conditional sales contracts are excluded from this definition.)

As you can see, the computation of the amount of benefits you may be entitled to is complex, but the important thing to remember is that the size of your family net income, your marital status and the number of children you have. All will affect your monthly Child Tax Benefit. For these reasons, a visit to your tax professional before you begin a conjugal relationship can help you determine how your monthly income will be affected by this decision. It can also really pay to reduce your family net income with RRSPs and other legitimate tax deductions in an attempt to qualify for or increase a Child Tax Benefit (CTB) payment.

35 TAKE THE TIME TO CALCULATE THE TAX-FREE SAVINGS POTENTIAL

Once you receive your CTB eligibility statement from Revenue Canada, take the time to calculate the potential tax-free accumulations you can save for your child's university, first house, car, etc. with the CTB working for you. Take our common-law couple, Jody and Mark, as an example.

Each earns $12,000 annually at their respective jobs. Filing a tax return could reap CTBs of about $125 each month for their baby, Angie, assuming no child care expenses are claimed. That amounts to about $1,500 each year until the child turns 7, if all things remain equal. From age 7 to 18, the monthly amount drops to about $100 a month or $1,200 a year. If this is saved faithfully (and all other factors relating to income and number of children remain the same), a fund well over $20,000 plus earnings could be accumulated by the child in 18 years. All earnings would be taxed in her hands, provided the amounts were deposited to a separate account used only for CTB deposits. What a way to split income and send Angie off — virtually tax free — on the road to success!

36 CLAIM DEPENDENTS OVER 18 WHO ARE INFIRM

If you support a person over the age of 18 who is mentally or physically infirm, you will qualify to make a newly enhanced tax credit claim on your tax return. It is not necessary for the dependant to be so severely incapacitated that daily living activities are markedly restricted. However, the disability must restrict the dependent from being self-supporting. Persons over the age of 65 are generally considered to be claimable by virtue of their age and infirmity. Net income of the dependant will be a restricting factor in making this claim.

Even if you are claiming an amount for dependants over 18 who are infirm, be sure also to file a tax return individually for these dependants to tap into their rightful GST Credit.

In 1997 the maximum tax credit is $2,353, and the dependant can have a net income of $4,103 before the credit is reduced.

37 TRANSFER TAX CREDITS FROM ONE SPOUSE TO ANOTHER

Spouses, including common-law spouses, should always prepare their taxes simultaneously. The lower earner's return is prepared first and, as mentioned, that person should file for the GST Credit for the family to create income "in his or her own right."

Once this return is completed you can quickly identify whether the spouse's net income is too high for a claim under the Spousal Amount. If the spouse is taxable, will an RRSP contribution bring about a non-taxable status? Does the spouse have RRSP contribution room: if so, is there still time for the spouse to contribute? (RRSP contributions must be made during the year or within the first 60 days of the year end.) Is there a better benefit if the higher earner contributes to the RRSP? (See Tip 40.)

If the spouse is not taxable, determine whether the higher-income earner can transfer any available age amount, pension income amount, tuition or education amount or disability amount to his or her own return. Find out by completing a Revenue Canada Schedule 2.

If the lower earner is taxable, consider claiming medical expenses on that person's return. This could increase the family tax refund, because medical expenses are reduced by 3% of net income. Then the new Refundable Medical Expense Supplement is calculated. Spouses are considered to be agents of each other for the purposes of the medical expenses, charitable donations or political contributions made by either, so group and claim them to the family's best tax benefit.

38 USE REVENUE CANADA'S ATTRIBUTION RULES TO YOUR ADVANTAGE

Except in very specific instances, earnings generated from principal that was transferred from a high-income earner to the spouse or a minor will generally be taxed in the hands of the transferor. This is true of interest, dividends or capital gains income earned on money transferred to your spouse, or interest and dividends earned on money transferred to your minor child.

For example, if you give your spouse $5,000 to invest in a Canada Savings Bond, the resulting interest is taxed back in your hands. You can avoid these rules if you can establish that the income should be properly attributed to the spouse, who had income "in his or her own right."

Income "earned in your own right" includes income from your own employment or self-employment, inheritances received, or income tax refunds or credits such as the Child Tax Benefit or Goods and Services Tax Credit. So, rather than spend that monthly Child Tax Benefit, have the lower-income earner invest it. The resulting investment earnings will be taxed in the lower earner's hands.

39 LET OTTAWA CREATE INCOME FOR THE SPOUSE OR CHILD

The key to maximizing refundable tax credits such as the Child Tax Benefit, the Goods and Services Tax Credit, the new Refundable Medical Expense Supplement or provincial tax credits is to reduce family net income with all legitimate tax deductions available. Have the lower-income earner apply for the refundable tax credits for the family. You can request the amounts to be electronically deposited directly to a bank account set up for investment purposes. Any resulting earnings on this investment are properly taxed to the lower-income earner.

Use the same method to create income for your child. Have the Child Tax Benefit directly deposited to a bank account in the name of the child. This an excellent way to start a university fund — you can split income and save tax dollars, too. (See Tip 35.)

40 BUY AN RRSP IN THE NAME OF YOUR SPOUSE

Looking down the road a bit, perhaps you are aware that your spouse will not have the same level of taxable pension income when you both retire. Your family unit ultimately pays more tax in this case because the majority of pension accumulations are in the hands of one spouse, who probably is in a higher tax bracket than the other spouse.

Plan to split RRSP accumulations in retirement by depositing your RRSP contribution in the name of your spouse, to balance out accumulations in each person's hands. You'll get the tax deduction, but your lower-earning spouse will be taxed on subsequent withdrawals, provided the money stays in the plan at least three years from the date of the last spousal RRSP contribution.

41 NO SPOUSE? BUY AN RRSP FOR YOUR CHILD

If you are a single parent, you can provide your child with the money to buy an RRSP, which shelters the earnings within the plan from the tax man until the amounts are withdrawn. As the child will not likely withdraw the amounts before age 18, resulting earnings are taxable in the child's hands. There is a catch here: the child must have "earned income" in the immediate prior year, or unused RRSP contribution room to qualify to make RRSP contributions. So, if your child has a part-time job, babysits or has a paper route, always be sure to file a tax return for him or her to create the necessary RRSP contribution room, especially since unused RRSP room can now be carried forward indefinitely. The child may not contribute any amount above the RRSP Contribution Room limit.

42 FILE A TAX RETURN FOR TEENAGERS

Always file a tax return for any family member who is earning a part-time income from employment or self-employment. Take 13-year-old Shannon, for example, who last year earned $50 each week looking after the neighbours' children after school. This translates into $2,500 after 50 weeks of work, and 18% of this amount qualifies for contribution to Shannon's RRSP. That's $450.

Why would you want to calculate this figure if she is not taxable and the RRSP contribution is not needed?

It's simple: If Shannon earns the same income every year for five years until she turns 18, she will have accumulated $2250 in unused RRSP contribution room. To register this amount of "room" with Revenue Canada, she must have filed a tax return for every year — in this case as a self-employed child care-giver. (She may also qualify for some lucrative deductions.)

At age 19, Shannon finds a full-time job and earns $18,000. She can now make an RRSP contribution of $2,250, which will save her approximately 28% (depending upon which province she lives in) or $630 in taxes. Very worthwhile indeed.

43 LOAN YOUR SPOUSE OR CHILD MONEY TO MAKE AN INVESTMENT

You can make a loan to your spouse or minor child to make an interest or dividend-bearing investment with the resulting earnings taxed to that spouse or child, if you follow the proper procedures. That is, a loan that bears a commercial rate of interest — calculated, charged and actually paid each year within 30 days of year end — is considered "legitimate," and resulting earnings are taxed in the spouse's or child's hands. Be sure also to provide for repayment terms.

Remember, the key to income splitting is to have the lower earners in the family invest, rather than spend, their income.

44 REINVEST SECOND-GENERATION EARNINGS

Earnings generated by investment income that was previously attributed is taxed to the lower-income earner. For example, if a father gave his daughter $10,000 to invest in a Guaranteed Investment Certificate, the resulting earnings would be taxed to him. However, if the interest earnings themselves were reinvested by the daughter in another investment (perhaps a Canada Savings Bond), the offsetting income from that second investment would be properly taxed to the daughter. This is called "second-generation earnings."

45 BUY A BUSINESS FOR YOUR SPOUSE OR CHILD

Business income earned from dollars or property transferred from the higher earner to the spouse or minor child is exempt from the attribution rules. This means the spouse or child may earn, and be taxed upon, the profits of the company. However, in the case of a spouse only, the profits on the sale of capital assets acquired directly from the higher-income earner would be attributed back to the higher-income earner.

46 GIVE A GIFT — TAX FREE

Feel free to give to your minor child or grandchild, niece or nephew or other child with whom you are related or dealing "at arm's length." Only interest and dividend earnings that result from your gift are taxed back to you.

There are no tax consequences if the child spends the money on consumer goods, pays for education or acquires a tax exempt principal residence, or a capital asset, such as a mutual fund that will result in a capital gain.

47 BUY CAPITAL ASSETS IN THE NAME OF YOUR CHILD OR GRANDCHILD

Yes, you read correctly. You can avoid the Attribution Rules by giving your minor child or grandchild a capital asset, such as a capital stock or mutual fund. The profit on the sale of the asset, or capital gain, is attributed to the child. Resulting capital gains will likely be taxed at a much lower tax rate in the hands of the child, if at all. On subsequent dispositions, be sure to take into account any Capital Gains Elections made on behalf of the child's accrued asset valuations in his or her 1994 tax return.

Unfortunately, dividends or "other income" earned on the capital stock gifted to a minor child are attributed back to the donor.

48 SAY ADIEU IN TAX HARMONY

You have learned that when you marry during the tax year, the Spousal Amount is based on net income for the entire year. If you separate or become divorced, however, use only the net income of your spouse up to date of separation. For tax purposes, this makes a good argument for separating in the early months of the tax year. Remember, should you reconcile and live together again before year end, Revenue Canada will consider you to be married for the whole year, in which case the spouse's net income for the whole year must again be used.

Common-law spouses, on the other hand, are subject to a "90-day rule." If, for example, you separated 90 days or more into the year, you are not considered to be "spouses" anymore for the purposes of the Income Tax Act. But, if you reconcile before year end, you are considered "spouses" again, with all of the relevant tax provisions intact, if you previously cohabited together for a full 12-month period. However, if you have a natural or adoptive child together, cohabitation on December 31 is enough to invoke the "spousal status."

As you can see, justifying your Spousal Amount claims could be an interesting challenge. If your personal life is that complicated, consider keeping a detailed documentation in a "relationship log"! The onus of proof is on you.

49 CERTAIN SUPPORT PAYMENTS ARE TAX DEDUCTIBLE TO THE PAYOR

New in '97

If you are considering a separation or divorce, there is important planning news regarding the taxation of child support payments made after

May 1, 1997: Child support payments will no longer be taxable to the recipient or deductible by the payor for new agreements in place after April 30, 1997. However, Spousal Support payments will still be considered taxable to the recipient and tax deductible to the payor.

Under the old rules, (agreements in place before May 1, 1997), amounts paid for the support of the spouse or children of a failed union depended upon the existence of all the following circumstances:

1. Amounts must be paid for the maintenance of the spouse or children, or both.
2. The spouses must be living apart at the time the payments were made and throughout the remainder of the year.
3. The parties must be separated and amounts paid pursuant to a divorce, judicial separation or written separation agreement.
4. Amounts paid must be paid on a periodic basis.
5. Amounts are deductible if paid in the year or the immediately preceding year. (In the latter case, adjust the prior-filed return.)

The old system of income inclusion and payment deductions will stay in effect for all child support agreements in place before May 1, 1997 unless:

1. Both parents jointly elect to have such agreements cease to apply as of an agreed upon date on or after May 1, 1997 (file Form T1157).
2. The amount of child support is changed by a court order or agreement made on or after May 1, 1997, (file form T1158) or
3. The court order specifically says the new tax rules will apply to payments on or after May 1, 1997.

Read new Form T1156 from Revenue Canada for additional details.

50 LEGAL FEES IN FAMILY DISPUTES MAY BE TAX DEDUCTIBLE

While the costs of obtaining a divorce or separation are not tax deductible, any amounts expended on legal fees to enforce the payment of previously established financial commitments are allowed.

If in the various legal proceedings the court orders the recipient to make a repayment of separation allowances previously received, the amounts so repaid are tax deductible in the current year and either of the two following years, if the amounts were previously taxable.

51   TAXABLE ALIMONY/MAINTENANCE INCOME QUALIFIES FOR RRSP PURPOSES

The recipient of taxable child support or spousal support payments is required to add them to income and pay tax at the applicable marginal tax rate. Here is some bad news: this income may necessitate the payment of quarterly tax instalments to Revenue Canada to avoid interest charges. You may be able to reduce or avoid these instalments entirely if you make a contribution to an RRSP. Taxable alimony/maintenance payments received in the immediately prior year will create RRSP contribution room which will reduce the amount of tax you pay on this income.

The payor of these support amounts, incidentally, must reduce his or her RRSP earned income for RRSP purposes by the amount of the Alimony/Maintenance deduction taken.

If you are now receiving tax-free Child Support, your RRSP contribution in future years will be reduced, while those who lost their Child Support deduction through these tax changes can take comfort in the fact that their RRSP Room will generally increase.

52   SPOUSAL SUPPORT PLANNING CAN BE PROFITABLE

As mentioned, payments made for spousal support in agreements negotiated after April 30, 1997 will continue to be taxable to the recipient and deductible to the payor.

In cases where the recipient has little or no income, it may be an idea to structure the agreement to receive taxable spousal support of at least $6,456 (the Basic Personal Amount) plus any RRSP contribution room available (based on last year's earned income) to keep the receipts tax free. (This assumes the recipient would actually make the allowable RRSP contributions.) The balance of the payments, if any, could be structured as tax-free child support after April 30, 1997.

53   MOVING EXPENSES ARE TAX DEDUCTIBLE

A relationship breakdown could precede a family move. If you are looking at such a circumstance, there are numerous tax-planning options to be aware of.

First, Canadians are taxed at their province of residence as at December 31 of the tax year. So, if you are considering a move to a province that has higher tax rates than the one you currently live in, plan the move early in the next year, if possible. If you move before year end, your income from the whole year will be taxed at the new province's rate, which will usually result in a tax liability at year end because those rates will not be reflected in your employer's remittance requirements.

The opposite is true if you are moving to a province with lower tax rates. Try to make this move before year end so that all of your income for the year is taxed at those lower tax rates.

Second, save all receipts pertaining to the move, including real estate commissions paid on the sale of your old residence and removal expenses, costs of meals and lodging en route and up to 15 days' temporary living accommodations in the new location, all provided you moved at least 40 kilometres closer to a new work location from your old metropolitan area. (This 40 kilometres is measured as the distance between the new work location and the old, using the shortest possible normal route of travel.) The tax deduction for moving expenses can be lucrative if you moved to start a job, a business or go to post-secondary school full-time at the new location.

✸ 54 RESP SAVINGS OPPORTUNITIES INCREASE

If you are looking for ways to shelter savings for your child's education, you may wish to look into the merits of a Registered Educational Savings Plan. Starting in 1997, the annual limit on the amount of total contributions to a RESP for each beneficiary increased to the lesser of $4,000 per year to a lifetime maximum of $42,000 per student.

While contributions made have no tax consequences for the contributor (i.e., the amounts are not tax deductible), the accumulations of earnings on the investment are not taxed until distribution to the student in the future. At that time, the earnings are reported by the student as an "educational assistance payment." Because these increased RESP contribution limits may eventually serve to increase the student's income in the future, tax returns should be filed by all young persons with part-time earnings. This is to build up RRSP contribution room, which can be used to offset the student's taxable income in the future.

Starting in 1998, should the student decide not to go to post-secondary school, RESP income may be returned to the contributor if the amounts have accumulated in the plan for at least 10 years. Such withdrawals will be reported as income, unless the contributor has RRSP contribution room, in which case up to $40,000 in tax-sheltered income accumulations may be transferred to the RRSP. If RESP income is not fully offset by RRSP deductions, a penalty tax of 20% will apply to the unsheltered RESP income.

55 THINK AHEAD

You should always have your family's financial legacy in mind when you prepare income tax returns. Are your assets protected if something should happen to you? How will the transfer of the cottage, your business, or other assets be affected by tax rules if you die? Will your child still be able to go to college? Will your spouse know how to invest your money or where your safety deposit box is? Proper tax planning includes a review of all of these tax questions, a review of your will, a review of your tax-free life insurance policy benefit provisions, and a review of your wishes and concerns, once your return is safely "put to bed" for another tax year.

CHAPTER 4

TAX-WISE TIPS
FOR STUDENTS

Do you know...

* *Teenagers should file tax returns every year and report every dollar earned...*
* *18% of all earned income by the child creates RRSP contribution room...*
* *Tuition and education tax credits can help both the student and the parents...*
* *Every 19-year-old should file their own return to claim the GST Credit...*
* *Child care and moving expenses can be claimed by a student...*
* *A $500 tax exemption is available on bursary or scholarship income...*

———————

The single-most significant wealth-creating opportunity a young adult has over any other taxpayer is *time*: time for interest-compounding to take effect on investment growth, and time to weather the economic cycles of the global community.

Ask some young adults for their vision for financial security, and they might reply, "To be a millionaire." Ask them how they'll achieve this goal, and they might say, "By winning a lottery!"

The goal, fortunately, is achievable; the method, however, is a long shot.

It is not unusual to think that every 18-year-old has the potential to be a millionaire, based on his or her own productivity and that of the money that will be saved. In fact, the "Lifetime Millionaire" is really an average Canadian...a taxpayer who makes $25,000 a year on average over a productive lifetime of 40 years, will have made one million dollars. Under today's tax rates, roughly one-third of that will be taxed away — close to $300,000.

Every parent can set his or her child on the road to financial freedom by teaching basic financial planning concepts, including how to use tax laws to their advantage. If each taxpayer could arrange their affairs to reduce their lifetime tax bill by just 10% — $30,000 in the example above — a lifestyle improvement would result. There are simple steps to begin your child's journey to lifetime tax savings:

- plan to accumulate a university fund with Child Tax Benefit Savings
- plan to create wealth by transferring capital assets to children at an early age
- teach your child to win the tax game...starting with the first play.

Take Bailey, for example. A 20-year-old engineering student, she is in receipt of income from a variety of sources: "scholarships" from a Registered Educational Savings Plan (RESP), scholarships from her university, a research grant, and even some income from part-time employment. Bailey should file her own separate tax return to claim her GSTC Credit, any provincial refundable tax credits she may be entitled to, the determination of available RRSP room so that a contribution may be made to offset scholarship, investment, and employment income, and finally, the computation of tuition and educational credits, which might be transferable to her parent's return.

The idea, therefore, is to get Bailey's income below the basic personal amount ($6,456) with all her available tax provisions (deductions for the first $500 of scholarship income, RRSP, investment carrying charges, non-refundable tax credits for CPP premiums, Employment Insurance, tuition, education credits, medical expenses, charitable donations, and so on) in order to create a transfer up to $5,000 of unused tuition and educational credits for her supporting individuals. These strategies will save the family unit hundreds, if not thousands, of dollars.

56 REPORT TIPS AND GRATUITIES

Students often work a summer or part-time stint as a waiter, waitress, bellhop, taxicab driver or other position in the personal services industry. Besides their wages, these employees must self-report any tips they make during the course of their employment.

Not only will these income sources create RRSP contribution room (see Tip 57), they are also eligible for CPP contributions that the taxpayer can make on a "self-remittance" basis through the tax return. Only teenagers 18 and over can contribute to the CPP; however, this is an excellent way to bolster your future retirement or disability pension plan draw.

By the way, for those "under" 18-year-olds who had CPP premiums deducted at source in error, an overpayment calculation can be completed via the tax return to recover these amounts to you.

 # 57 FILE A RETURN FOR CURRENT AND FUTURE TAX REFUNDS

Every dollar earned, whether by a paper route, pizza delivery, babysitting, or any other part-time job you have had throughout your adolescence, should be reported on a tax return every year to create "RRSP contribution room," in the event that you may wish to contribute to an RRSP. You should therefore file a return even if the income earned is too low to be taxable.

Sometime in the future, when earnings may be large enough to be taxable, the RRSP room can be used to create an RRSP deduction. Such a move will not only save tax dollars for the young worker in that year, but may create a tuition/education credit transfer of up to $5,000 for a student's parents or spouse. In addition, the tax-sheltered compounding of this fund within the RRSP will grow into a significant retirement fund for that young person over time (see Tip 58). RRSP room can now be carried forward indefinitely.

In order to contribute to an RRSP you must have had "earned income" sometime in the past. Unfortunately many students find they are prohibited from contributing to an RRSP in the first year they are taxable, because the required "RRSP Room" does not exist. If you can rectify this by filing returns for past years in which you had part-time earnings, do so. It can help you create tax savings for yourself and your supporting individuals.

Finally, remember that even if you are not taxable, filing a tax return might help you collect on the new Refundable Medical Expense Supplement. (See Tip 204.) So save all those receipts for glasses, contact lenses, dental work, etc.

✹ 58 CONTRIBUTE TO AN RRSP AS SOON AS POSSIBLE

There are two reasons most people contribute to an RRSP — the first is to receive an offsetting tax deduction that will reduce taxes payable. The second is to accumulate tax free earnings within the RRSP. In the case of students, some planning is necessary to maximize these benefits.

If the student has taxable income (that is, income exceeding the Basic Personal Amount) and the available "RRSP Room," a contribution to the RRSP should be made. The student can then decide how much of an RRSP deduction to claim. In general you would want to claim enough of the contribution to bring taxable income down below the Basic Personal Amount. That would enable the transfer of tuition and education credits to supporting persons, or starting in the 1997 tax year, the carry forward of such credits to future years of higher earnings. The rest of the RRSP contribution can also be carried forward for use in future tax years. In determining the amount of the RRSP deduction, the student should also take into account the optimum net income level to maximize refundable tax credits such as the GST Credit and the new Refundable Medical Expense Supplement. That's good tax planning.

Investments inside an RRSP make so much sense for a young Canadian. The person who contributes money to an RRSP each year for 40 years, starting at age 20, will likely have the opportunity to accumulate more wealth, even though they invest less money, than their middle-aged counterparts.

In a simplistic example, at an interest rate of 6%, the 20-year-old who contributes $1,000 each year — less than $85 a month — will accumulate $154,761.97 on principal investments of $40,000. The 40-year-old who contributes $333 a month or $4,000 each year for 20 years (or twice the principal–$80,000) will have only $147,142.36.

The net gain, before acknowledging the tax savings made over the years, is almost $48,000 in favour of the 20-year-old: about $7600 more in overall accumulations, but accomplished with only half the principal investment. The elements of time, rate of return, and tax-free compounding within the RRSP, used to your best advantage, will accelerate your financial freedom, particularly if you start investing early in your lifetime.

59 EARN INTEREST INCOME INSIDE AN RRSP

Because of the heavy marketing activities during the "RRSP season," most Canadians have heard of RRSPs and understand that they are a good idea for reducing taxes and creating security in retirement. Many Canadians, however, don't understand the difference between investing inside and outside of an RRSP.

If you place your investments inside a "registered account" it means that you will likely claim a tax deduction for the full amount of the principal invested (depending on the size of your RRSP contribution room, however). You are making your investment on a pre-tax basis, in other words. The earnings that your investments make within the plan are sheltered until you withdraw the funds. Then both principal and earnings are included in income.

When you invest in a non-registered account, you are investing with tax-paid dollars. Subsequent earnings are taxed as earned, and withdrawals of principal are not reported on the return.

For these reasons, there is an ordering of choices within your investment vehicles that makes logical tax sense. Those who have taxable incomes and RRSP room, for example, should contribute to an RRSP first — provided they are not restricted by age. (You cannot contribute to an RRSP in the year you turn 70 unless you contribute to the RRSP of a younger spouse.) That's because you'll receive an immediate return on your investment through tax savings on your return.

Once you have made the decision to invest regularly in an RRSP, it is important to choose the individual investments inside the plan carefully. Your tax sheltered interest earnings, for example, will multiply faster when compared with results from an unsheltered interest-bearing investment outside the RRSP. This is because compound interest earnings outside an RRSP must be reported on the tax return on an annual basis — even though you don't actually receive the money until the principal is withdrawn and interest is paid out to you. A tax bite is taken from all such earnings, in advance, if your income otherwise exceeds the Basic Personal Amount, deductions and credits.

On the other hand, Canadian dividend or capital gains-bearing assets might be held outside the RRSP umbrella, to take advantage of lower tax rates on these earnings types.

60 CONSIDER OVER-CONTRIBUTING TO YOUR RRSP

To maximize the tax-free growth of earnings inside an RRSP, you may wish to consider contributing more than your "RRSP Room." This is allowed, but with some restrictions. That is, you should plan to keep the over-contribution balance under $2,000, to avoid penalties. You must also be over 18 years old to make an over-contribution.

However, there is another catch: be sure that in the future you will have the required RRSP contribution room to "use up" these extra RRSP contributions. Without that room, which is based on "earned income" from the immediately preceding tax years, no RRSP deduction is allowed. In fact you could face double taxation if the over-contribution remains undeducted: principal and interest is still taxable upon withdrawal, even though you never benefited from an RRSP deduction for the principal contributed.

For a young taxpayer, however, the over-contribution strategy can make sense, assuming that person will be working at a job or gainful self-employment after graduation.

61 MAXIMIZE THE USE OF THE BASIC PERSONAL AMOUNT

Under current rules, every person has a right to earn $6,456 — or $538 each month — before he or she is subject to tax. Many families waste this opportunity of cashing in on tax-free productivity. Four people earning $6,456 each can make $25,824 completely tax free every year, for example. Teach your family members to strive to earn at least this income ceiling every year to maximize wealth within the family unit.

There is much you can do to help. You may wish to hire that student in the family business, for example. Let's say the student earns $5,000. You can deduct this expense from business income, provided work was actually done by the student for a wage at fair market value. All of that income earned by the student is income tax free. In addition, resulting RRSP room is $900, which can be used next year to make an RRSP contribution. Tax-free earnings will start accumulating in the RRSP immediately, if the contribution is actually made. Further the RRSP of $900 will reduce taxes payable in the future. Even more tax savings may result with a transfer of tuition/education credits to one of the parents' returns.

As you see, the $5000 the student earns reaps tax savings in many different ways. Therefore, this circle of wealth creation begins with the personal productivity of each family member.

62 MINIMIZE TAX ON EDUCATIONAL PRIZES

Students who are scholars qualify for a special tax break.

Scholarships, fellowships and bursaries — including net project grants received by artists — qualify for a special tax exemption: the first $500 of such income is tax exempt. Scholarships are usually reported on a T4A slip and then entered on the tax return to Line 130, "Other Income."

Be sure to recover past overpayments if you forgot to claim the $500 exemption. You can do this by requesting an adjustment to your previously filed tax return.

63 STUDENTS QUALIFY FOR A TUITION FEE CREDIT

New in '97

Students who attend an educational institution providing courses at a post-secondary school level, or an institution certified by Human Resource Development Canada to provide occupational skills, may be eligible for the tuition fee tax credit, which is a non-refundable tax credit. Tuition fees paid must exceed $100 to be eligible for the write-off.

An educational institution may include a professional organization that provides educational courses to members, as long as one minimum qualification for membership is secondary school graduation.

Certain post-secondary institutes outside Canada may also qualify for the tuition fee credit provided that courses taken lead to a degree not lower than the bachelor or equivalent level. The course taken must be of not less than 13 consecutive weeks in duration.

The student must be at least 16 years old, and there is no upper limit to the size of the tuition fee credit, but the amount must exceed $100.

Tuition paid for part-time courses, such as night school, will also qualify, as do fees paid for correspondence courses, but in that case only if taken inside Canada.

Starting with the 1997 tax filing year, students who are not taxable may carry forward their unused tuition tax credits to future tax years, when the credits can be used to offset future taxes payable.

64 **MOST TUITION EXPENSES OF STUDENTS ARE TAX DEDUCTIBLE**

Students should be very careful to save receipts pertaining to their studies for use on their income tax returns, as outlined above.

Eligible tuition fees include admission fees, charges for use of a library, charges for use of labs, examination fees, application fees, confirmation fees, charges for certificates, academic fees, membership or seminar fees specifically related to an academic program and its administration, directly supervised flying time and lecture time for those studying to be commercial pilots.

Starting in the 1997 tax year, certain ancillary fees and charges, other than student association fees, will be allowed for the purposes of the tuition fee credit, provided that such fees are required from all full-time or part-time students. This can include athletic and health services fees. Specifically disallowed are fees levied in relation to property acquired by students, fees for the provision of financial assistance to students or fees for the construction or renovation of any building, unless that building or facility is owned by the institution and used to provide courses at a post-secondary level.

Also ineligible are fees paid for medical care, board and lodging, transportation, parking, tangible goods (slide rules, microscopes, uniforms, gowns), solo flying time, entrance fees to professional organizations or the cost of books, except those used in correspondence courses.

65 **TUITION FEES ARE DEDUCTIBLE FOR SESSIONS IN THE CALENDAR YEAR ONLY**

Even though you may pay for the tuition fees for your entire academic year in September, only those fees pertaining to studies in the calendar year (January to December) will be claimed on your current year's return.

Therefore, from both a tax and a cash flow point of view, it may make sense to pay tuition fees in instalments.

 66 **CLAIM THE MONTHLY EDUCATION CREDIT**

Students may claim $150 a month for each month or any part thereof that they were in full-time attendance at a designated educational institute, as a non-refundable tax credit on their 1997 income tax return.

(This is an increase from the $100 a month allowed on last year's tax return.) An exception to the full-time rule is made in the case of disabled persons, who by nature of their disability are able to take only a part-time load.

For planning purposes, you should also know that for the 1998 and subsequent tax years, this monthly education amount will be increasing to $200 a month.

A qualifying educational program for these purposes is one that runs for at least three consecutive weeks and requires instruction or work in the program of at least 10 hours a week. The work involved in the minimum 10 hours a week includes all forms of direct instruction such as lectures, practical training or laboratory work, as well as research time for the purpose of writing a thesis. Usually four full courses or more qualify, although three may qualify if the educational institute ensures the workload satisfies the 10-hour-per-week minimum. Work on essays, term papers and other written work and oral presentations will count.

Further, a registered student spending a majority of time researching for post-graduate studies will be regarded as being in full-time attendance, as will a post-graduate student holding a full-time job if the required research time is spent.

 ## 67 CLAIM THE EDUCATION CREDIT FOR TEACHERS

Most teachers taking summer school will be allowed to claim the new $150 a month education tax credit.

 ## 68 TRANSFER UNUSED TUITION FEES AND EDUCATION CREDITS

Students may transfer the unused portions of their tuition fee/education credits to a supporting spouse, parent or grandparent. However, they must first use the amount to reduce their own income to non-taxable status.

The maximum combined transferable amount is $5,000. No amount may be claimed by a spouse who, because of marriage breakdown, is living separately and apart from the student at the end of the year and for 90 days commencing in the new year.

Unmarried students, or married students whose spouse is not claiming the student for the Spousal Amount or any tuition/education tax credits, may transfer the unused amounts to the student's parent or grandparent. The student must designate in writing that the transfer is being made to that person (use Form T2202).

The "parent" can include in-laws, step-parents, natural parents, adoptive parents or someone the individual was wholly dependent upon for support and in whose custody the child was before reaching age 19. Not included are foster parents who received support payments for the child.

It is important to plan to take maximum advantage of the new tax rules for 1997 and future years. For example, now that students can carry forward unused tuition and education credits for use on their own future tax returns, a new question must be asked: is it better to take the tax benefits from the transfer of tuition and education credits to a parent's or spouse's return now, or forfeit those savings in favour of future tax reductions in the student's own hands, later? Also, never transfer more tuition/education credits than your supporting person needs to reduce income, because now any balance can be carried forward.

Given that we are in a period of extraordinarily high tax rates today, supporting individuals and their students might wish to split the benefits of tax savings now, and invest the difference.

 ## 69 FILE FOR GST/HST CREDITS TO HELP WITH NON-DEDUCTIBLE DEBT

If you are age 19 or older, married, or a parent, you may claim a GST/HST Credit in your own right, simply by filing an income tax return. You must also be a resident of Canada as at December 31 of the tax year, to qualify. You must not have been in prison for six months or more during the tax year.

If you missed making the claim in a prior year, file now and Revenue Canada will refund the missed credit to you. You can then take those tax refunds and pay off your non-deductible student loans, credit cards or invest in an RRSP or other investment.

 ## 70 STUDENTS SHOULD CLAIM CHILD CARE EXPENSES

Child care expenses may be claimed on behalf of expenditures for the student's child, incurred while the student was in school, to offset income from employment, self-employment, a training allowance under the National Training Act or a research grant.

There are also special tax calculations for those parents who are attending school but who may not have actively earned income sources.

The basic rules of the claim are the following:

For most taxpayers, the claim for child care expenses, made on line 214 of the tax return, is a maximum of either $3,000 or $5,000 per child, depending on the age of the child and whether the child is severely disabled, the earned income sources of the parent, and the actual amounts spent on child care. Usually it is the lower-income earner in the family who is required to claim child care expenses, but when a parent attends post-secondary school, it is possible for the higher-income earner to make the claim, based on that person's actively earned income and a maximum weekly amount of either $150 or $90, depending on the age of the child, and/or infirmity.

The maximum age of children for whom child care expense may be deducted is "under 16 at any time during the year." The higher deduction limits are for those children under the age of 7 or severely disabled (that is when a Disability Tax Credit is claimable for the child). The lower limits are for those between the ages of 7 and 16, or mentally or physically infirm (but no Disability Tax Credit is claimed).

Where the tax filer attends a designated educational institute that qualifies for the education tax credit, or attends a secondary school (i.e., a high school) in a program of at least 3 consecutive weeks' duration, requiring at least 10 hours per week in work in the program, a maximum deduction of $150 a week for each child under age 7 will be allowed (this includes severely disabled children at any age), or $90 a week for those over 6 and under 16, even if the student has no actively earned income sources.

Rather, in those cases, the claim is based on total income sources — active or inactive — reported at line 236 of the tax return (calculated as if no child care expenses were claimed). This means that those who receive only investment income, taxable alimony/maintenance/child support payments, Employment Insurance, or Social Assistance, will be able to make a tax deductible claim for child care expenses. (It is important to note that those who now receive tax-free child support may see an effect on this part of the tax return.)

The resulting claim for child care will decrease net income, and thereby increase other refundable tax credits (such as the GST Credit or provincial tax credits) claimed elsewhere on the return of the student or the supporting individuals.

Under these new rules, which were introduced on the 1996 tax return, it is possible that a new child care claim may be created for a couple, provided that they were both enrolled in a designated educational program at the same time (for at least one week) and two-thirds of earned income is lower than the total child care expenses paid, the maximum deduction available and the normal weekly restrictions for the higher-income earner.

The taxpayer must obtain a special tax form (T778) to make the claim, and, because these rules are new and fairly complicated, take your time in making the claim, or consider obtaining professional help.

71 STUDY MOVING EXPENSE RULES FOR STUDENTS

Students may also qualify for special tax treatment under the provision for moving expenses, a tax deduction that will again reduce the net income on Line 236. If you move to start a summer job, for example, your moving expenses may be tax deductible against those employment earnings, providing you move to take a job which is at least 40 kilometres away from your old residence.

The same rules hold true if you move after graduation to take a job in a new city, or if you move to a university or other post-secondary school — inside or outside of Canada — to study under a scholarship or fellowship, research grant or other similar award.

Foreign students who are residents of Canada may deduct moving expenses from taxable award income received in Canada.

Deductible moving expenses include the cost of selling the former residence, such as real estate commissions, penalties for paying off a mortgage before maturity and legal fees and advertising costs, expenses associated with the new home purchase such as transfer taxes and legal fees, temporary living accommodations for up to 15 days including hotel and the full cost of meals, all removal and transportation expenses for moving the household and all family members and the costs of cancelling an unexpired lease.

Non-deductible moving expenses include losses on the sale of the home, house-hunting trips and expenses to clean a rented residence.

Be sure to keep all receipts, because moving expenses are often audited, and are very lucrative in reducing income in the year of the move, or future years, if there is an excess of expenses over income earned in the new location.

CHAPTER 5

TAX-WISE EMPLOYMENT NEGOTIATIONS

Do you know...

* *Employees have the option of negotiating for remuneration of both cash and benefits...*
* *Tax-free benefits may be a better option than a cash raise...*
* *Your company car is a taxable benefit, but certain car allowances are tax free...*
* *Employees are allowed to claim some out-of-pocket expenses on the return...*
* *The GST rebate on tax deductible expense is missed by most taxpayers...*

It's true. Most people think that the person who has only one T4 slip has a relatively simple tax calculation. Truth is, if your tax return is that simple, you're probably overpaying your taxes and under-utilizing wealth-creating opportunities. It is a mistake to get lulled into the belief that tax-filing simplicity and the minimization of your tax liability are linked. Unfortunately, complexity and tax savings are. You or your tax professional may have to run through a few extra tax-filing hoops to arrange your affairs within the framework of the law to pay only the correct amount of tax. However, an understanding of slightly more involved tax provisions and how you can best use them to your own advantage can make a huge difference in your after tax position.

Most taxpayers find that it's worth it to get involved in knowing more about your tax-filing rights today, and the provisions that can help you pay less tax in the future.

An employee has lots of opportunity to maximize the investment made in the employer–employee relationship. The first thing you'll want to do is find ways to minimize the source deductions your employer must make for income taxes, to utilize all provisions that bring tax free benefits your way, to claim all legitimate deductions available for any of your out-of-pocket employment expenses, to invest your tax savings, and to negotiate your employment contract to maximize all monetary opportunities for wealth creation — including taxable benefits, profit sharing, and the like.

When it comes to your tax affairs, don't wait for the ship to come in. Row out a ways to meet it!

New in '97 72 REPORT INCOME FROM MISSING INFORMATION SLIPS

If you have lost an information slip, such as a T4 slip, dig out the cheque stubs or other proof of payment of salary or wages. This income, even if only casual in nature, must still be reported by the taxpayer. It is also important to do so, to create RRSP contribution room which may be used to the taxpayer's advantage in future years. The onus is on the taxpayer to report all income from employment, whether or not a T4 Slip is received.

In the case of investors, it will be easy to identify which institutions have not sent out a slip — there is no requirement for the institution to do so unless the amounts are over $50 — so check all banking records for unreported earnings. Also acquire annual statements from your stockbroker to record information relating to stock or mutual fund and bond transactions. Look back at prior-filing habits, current year's bank books, last year's Notice of Assessment from Revenue Canada as well as current year's bank statements to report all income received. If you previously made a Capital Gains Election, carry forward information about the new value of your assets or "exempt gains balances" of mutual funds. Finally, new in 1997, if you receive funds or property from a non-resident trust, or are indebted to one, you may have to file a new tax form on or before your normal filing due date, to report the details.

73 YOU CAN NEGOTIATE FOR CASH OR BENEFITS

If you are negotiating your own employment contract, as most employees do, be sure you know all the tax rules —- and be aware that cash is not your only possible remuneration.

The most successful negotiator is not necessarily one who wins it all, but rather one who aims for a win-win settlement. That's why a knowledge of tax-free and taxable benefits can be so lucrative in an employment negotiation. Your employer may be unable to give you a raise but could be quite agreeable to a number of "perks" that will raise your standard of living.

74 TAX-FREE BENEFITS ARE NICE

Tax-free perks are, of course, the best kind! Consider negotiating for:

- discounts on merchandise
- uniforms or special on-the-job clothing
- employee counselling for health, retirement or re-employment
- employer-paid costs for an attendant if employee is severely impaired by injury
- subsidized meals
- transportation to and from work
- membership at an athletic or social club.
- relocation expenses

When a raise is out of the question, or the cash a company can offer you is already at its maximum level, it may be easier for your employer to grant you one of these wishes.

75 TAX-FREE AUTO ALLOWANCES CAN PAY OFF

If, under the contract of your employment, you are required to use your car, there are certain instances when an auto allowance, paid to you by your employer, can be received on a completely tax-free basis. For example, if the auto allowance:

(1) is based solely on the number of miles or kilometres you drive to meet your obligations under your contract of employment;

(2) the amount is reasonable; and

(3) no other reimbursement is received to cover auto costs. However, the employer may pay your costs of supplementary business insurance, parking, toll, and ferry charges without affecting the tax-free status of your auto allowance.

Therefore, the wise employee will submit a detailed auto log to the employer very year in order to validate the tax-free status of his or her auto allowance.

76 BIRTHDAY GIFTS CAN BE TAX FREE

One interesting perk of employment can be the receipt of a gift in the amount of up to $100 from your employer. Such a gift can be received tax free once a year, except in the year of marriage, when a $200 tax-free gift can be received. Unfortunately, the employer will not be entitled to a write-off for the amount either.

Still, leaving hints about your upcoming birthday every year could pay off, if your employer is tax wise...

77 TAXABLE BENEFITS ARE NOT BAD, EITHER

A taxable benefit is a tangible good or service received from your employer as a form of remuneration. It is reported on a T4, and included as total earnings in Box 14. The employer is required to take off the tax for these perks at the time the value is transferred to you, so you might be a little poorer on the cash side, but living a better lifestyle as a result. Timing is an issue, as is the present value of the perk received.

Negotiating and receiving a taxable benefit can be better, for example, than waiting to earn the after-tax dollars and buying the goods or services yourself. Your employer may be able to offer you the following perks:

- rent-free or low-rent housing
- employer-paid vehicle
- interest-free or low-interest loans
- income tax preparation services
- travel benefits for the family
- tuition fees
- financial counselling

- gifts of consumer goods
- group health or life insurance coverage.

78 FIND WAYS TO REDUCE INCOME TAX SOURCE DEDUCTIONS

Your employer is required by law to reduce your gross pay by certain statutory source deductions such as premiums payable to the Canada Pension Plan and Employment Insurance. In the case of income tax deductions, there is some flexibility in the amounts taken from your pay. The first step an employer will usually take is to have you complete a TD1 form. This form will tell the employer what non-refundable tax credits you will qualify for, and from this the tax withholding rate can be determined.

However, it is also possible to have tax withholding reduced during the year. Any time in which the taxpayer will have a significant number of other tax deductions on his or her personal tax return, he or she can apply to Revenue Canada to have source deductions reduced. This can happen if the following provisions will apply in the tax year:

a. Loss carryovers are available

b. The following deductions will be claimed:
   1. Registered Pension Plan deductions
   2. RRSP contributions
   3. Union Dues or professional fees
   4. Child Care Expenses
   5. Moving Expenses
   6. Allowable Business Investment Losses
   7. Employment Expenses
   8. Carrying Charges
   9. Repayments of EI, or other social benefits erroneously paid to you
   10. Alimony or Maintenance payments deductible
   11. Northern Residents Deductions
   12. Overseas Employment Tax Credits

c. Any other provisions that will reduce the taxpayer's taxable income

To reduce your tax withholdings and therefore increase your monthly income, a letter is forwarded to Revenue Canada, requesting that tax deductions be waived on the salary or wages, the name and address of the employer is outlined, and, in the case of alimony or RRSP contributions, the name of the recipient or plan holder is outlined. The employer will then receive a letter of authority from Revenue Canada waiving the requirement for tax deductions on the income in question. The process of obtaining the waiver takes about three weeks.

79   MOVING AT REQUEST OF EMPLOYER CAN PAY OFF

If your employer moves you to another part of the country, ask for an Employee Home Relocation Loan. This is an interest-free or low-interest loan designed to cushion the costs of housing at the new city. A taxable benefit will be calculated and included in your income, based on the difference between the current prescribed rate of interest set by Revenue Canada, and the interest rate you are paying for the loan.

An offsetting deduction is allowed on a portion of this taxable benefit for the value of the loan, up to $25,000, computed for a five-year period. This is a tax break that can be lucrative for the taxpayer. However, the most difficult part about this deduction may be finding an employer who'll agree to the plan!

Remember that unreimbursed moving expenses may qualify for a tax deduction. This could include the costs of removal and storage, travelling and transportation costs, costs associated with the new home purchase, such as transfer tax and legal fees, and costs of selling your old home, such as real estate commissions or penalties incurred when paying off a mortgage before maturity. It may be a wise move to work out the tax-saving details with a qualified tax professional before packing your bags.

80   SHOULD YOU TAKE THE CASH...OR THE CAR?

New in '97

Here's a common tax question: Is it better to take the cash, pay the tax and buy your own car, or should you negotiate for an employer-owned vehicle? What are the tax consequences when an employer pays for your auto operating costs? To answer these questions, it is important to understand the tax consequences which, unfortunately, are rather complicated.

When your employer provides a vehicle to you, a taxable benefit is computed for any time the vehicle is used by you or your family for "personal use." The benefit has two components: the value of the vehicle itself, and operating costs relating to the vehicle. While paying the tax on these benefits can sting come tax time, an employer-provided vehicle may be a faster way for you to drive a new car than waiting to accumulate enough after-tax dollars to buy one outright, or take on the risk of financing the purchase or lease yourself.

Where the employer owns the vehicle, the benefit is called the "standby charge," which is calculated as 2% per month (or 24% annually) of the original cost of the car. If the car is leased, the benefit is calculated as two-thirds of the leasing costs, without including the insurance costs.

If the employer also pays your operating expenses, a second taxable benefit is calculated based on the actual costs of operation relating to personal driving. For 1997, the operating benefits will be calculated at 14 cents per kilometre of personal driving or 11 cents if the principal business of the employee is selling autos, less any amounts the employee reimbursed the employer for operating expenses. (The reimbursement must occur within 45 days of the year end.)

Or, where the auto is used at least 50% of the time for employment purposes, the employee may elect to have 50% of the standby charge added to income, as an operating benefit, less any reimbursements of expenses paid back to the employer. Therefore, 3% per month (or 36% annually) of the original cost of the vehicle is calculated for both the employer-paid operating expenses and the value of the car, times the number of months the vehicle is available for personal use.

Finally, if the car is used at least 90% of the time for employment purposes, the standby charge could be reduced or eliminated if personal use is less than 1,000 kilometres per month. This provision could wipe out your taxable benefit entirely. Check this out with your tax professional, and read on.

81 CHOOSE THE EMPLOYER-PROVIDED VEHICLE

If you are provided with an employer-owned vehicle whose capital cost is $21,000, your taxable benefit each year will be $5,040 (24% of $21,000). If you are paying tax at a marginal rate of 42%, this benefit will cost you about $2,100.

If you are also provided with the operating costs, and qualify to choose the 50% of standby-charge election, your taxable benefit would be $7,560 with resulting taxes payable of $3,175.20.

The standby charge, by the way, is always computed on the original cost of the vehicle. Because it does not decrease as the vehicle depreciates, the standby charge can be expensive if you're driving an old car. In these cases, then, it is wiser to be driving a new car, to justify the tax costs. This should be part of your negotiation with your employer.

82 STANDBY CHARGES CAN BE REDUCED

If you use your employer-provided vehicle 90% or more for employment use, and your personal use is less than 1,000 kilometres each month, you can have your standby charge reduced, which will save you money. A special tax calculation will have to be made to justify personal use and submitted to your employer.

Simply take the usual standby charge and multiply it by the number of personal kilometres over 1,000 times the number of days in the month the car was available to you.

For example, let's say the normal standby charge is $5,040, and your personal use driving is only 500 kilometres a month. Your revised standby charge is $5,040 × 6000 km (personal kilometers driven in the year) divided by 12,000 (1000 kilometres per month). The result is a taxable standby charge of $2,520, assuming the car was available to you all year long.

The key to this lucrative tax saver is to keep track carefully of all personal/business driving.

New in '97 83 OR...ASK FOR HELP BUYING YOUR OWN CAR

One of the disadvantages of an employer-provided vehicle is what happens when you lose your job or the employer loses the business: no family car.

If this is a concern, you may wish to secure ownership of the family vehicle by asking either for a raise to cover your car payments, or an employer-provided low-interest loan with which to purchase the vehicle, or both.

The benefit of a low- or no-interest loan will be added to your income, and will be subject to tax at your normal marginal tax rate.

However, if you are required by your contract of employment to use your vehicle in your employment and pay all costs, an offsetting tax deduction is allowed for the employment portion of the interest benefit.

To buy a $25,000 car outright, you'll have to earn about $39,500 before tax, assuming a marginal tax rate of about 42% (25,000 × 1.58). If the vehicle's costs are tax deductible, by virtue of your employment contract, it may be wiser to finance the cost of the car, take a deduction for the interest costs — up to a maximum claimable amount of $250 a month or $8.33 a day in 1997 — and use the cash you now have to top up your RRSP. Then use your tax savings from the RRSP to pay down the car loan.

84 LEASING PROVIDES GREAT TAX WRITE-OFFS, BUT NO EQUITY

To some, perhaps the best tax benefits of all arise out of leasing a vehicle. But beware, Revenue Canada has just curtailed some of these benefits. In the past, leasing costs paid up to a maximum of $650 a month could be deducted (plus PST/GST), based on the proportion of employment/personal use that was made of the vehicle. This maximum has now been reduced to $550 a month (plus PST/GST) for new leases entered into in the 1997 tax year. Given that the capital cost allowance claim-based value of a purchased vehicle has increased to $25,000 (plus taxes) you should compare your lease costs to the combined interest and CCA deductions you would have received if you had purchased a vehicle instead.

You may find that the write-offs between an employee-owned and a leased vehicle are similar. However, there are two major differences: timing and return on investment. In year one, only one-half the normal depreciation rate (1/2 of 30%) is allowed on the owned vehicle, based on a maximum capital cost of $25,000 plus PST and GST, as mentioned previously. Therefore, the leased vehicle generally provides greater tax benefits in the first year, depending on when you acquire it during the year.

At the end of the term of the lease, however, you have no capital asset on your balance sheet. If this is of concern to you or your banker, consider investing your tax savings from the lease write-off in another income-producing asset that has potential for appreciation.

Some leases can be structured so that you "buy out" the asset for the amount of the last payment or other similarly small amount that makes it attractive for you to acquire ownership at the end of the lease term. Such an agreement may change the leasing agreement into a conditional sales agreement under which the periodic payments are considered "capital" rather than "operational," and are therefore not fully deductible. Watch out for this.

85 CONSIDER ALL VEHICLE ACQUISITION VARIABLES

The question of whether to buy, lease or negotiate an employer-provided vehicle should be viewed from a cash flow and investment viewpoint; there are many variables to be considered:

1. In general, with an employer-provided vehicle, a standby charge and operating benefit will hit your pocketbook at the very least the end of April in taxes due, or in the requirement to make quarterly instalment payments if your employer fails to make source deductions throughout the year. But you won't have to use your after-tax dollars to pay for operating expenses and financing costs incurred during the year.

2. Choose a self-leased vehicle and you'll generally have the bigger tax write-off in the first year, at least, but you must also consider that the lease costs and operating expenses must be paid throughout the year with your after-tax earnings: 50- to 60-cent dollars. A steady income and job security is required.

3. If you choose to own your vehicle, your cash flow may be improved over the leasing option, as you'll pay only operating costs and financing charges with after-tax dollars throughout the year. A portion of those operating costs may be recoverable on your tax return. You'll get a deduction for interest and capital cost allowance at year end, which compensates you for the depreciation, and you'll end up with an asset on the books to increase your net worth. If you use your tax savings to pay off your car loan, you'll also have the opportunity to save money on financing charges.*

   * Although you might consider paying off non-deductible debt or topping up your RRSP first.

Under Option One, you have the use of your pre-tax dollar until April 30, when you must have the money on hand to pay the tax liability. Under Option Two, you must have the income to finance the lease costs each month and wait to get back the tax benefits of your cash expenditures until you file your tax return. Under Option Three, you have to earn the after-tax dollars first before you can afford the car or have the means to finance the purchase.

How does one make the decision? Ask your tax professional to crunch the numbers under each scenario so you can be sure.

86 YOU CAN DEDUCT EXPENSES OF EMPLOYMENT

Employees enter into a master–servant relationship, which is firmly regulated by the Income Tax Act. In general, an employee is not allowed to make tax deductions from income unless it is a requirement of the contract of employment to make out-of-pocket expenditures that are unreimbursed.

Employees also cannot write off the cost of depreciable property, with the exception of capital cost allowance on automobiles, aircraft or musical instruments.

However, under certain circumstances, employment expenses are legitimate and tax deductible. If you are earning a salary, part salary, part commission or commission only, make sure you claim all your tax breaks. The first thing you have to do to make a claim, is to file Form T2200, "Declaration of Employment Conditions," which must be signed by the employer.

Take Mike, for example, a high school teacher who runs the continuing education department for the local high school, as well as his normal teaching duties in the woodworking and graphic arts department. He receives a salary of $65,000 a year plus a taxable car allowance of $1,500. At tax filing time, however, he finds his expenses have exceeded this allowance. For his car, including depreciation, expenses total $7,400; 50% of this is employment-related driving according to his auto log. There have also been expenses for meals and entertainment, and Mike is aware that 50% of his $950 in expenses can be claimed on his return. Finally, special supplies expenses, like wall-display materials, stationery, and other office supply items amounting to $350 were not reimbursed. So his eligible employment expenses amount to about $4,500, and at his tax bracket about half of this can be received back in tax savings...very worthwhile indeed.

There's more good news. Mike can also apply for a rebate of GST/HST paid on his income-tax deductible expenses. In fact, because Mike only just became aware of these tax provisions he can request an adjustment for missed employment expenses all the way back to 1985, as well as missed GST rebates back to 1991, the year this controversial tax came into effect.

Remember this, however: these claims will only be allowed if Form T2200 "Declaration of Employment Conditions" is signed by the employer and available with the rest of the schedules when filing your tax return, and all receipts are kept for presentation upon audit request.

87 ALLOWABLE EXPENSES FOR THOSE WHO EARN A SALARY

You may be able to claim the following expenses on your tax return if you are an employee who is paid an hourly wage or salary. To do so, complete Form T777, Statement of Employment Expenses. If you are an employed commissioned sales person you can claim the expenses listed below plus some additional ones, listed in Tip # 89:

- accounting and legal fees incurred to collect salary or wages
- motor vehicle expenses including capital cost allowances
- travelling expenses, including cost of meals if away for at least 12 hours from the municipality where your employer is located
- parking costs
- supplies used directly in your work
- salaries paid to a substitute or assistant
- office rent
- workspace in the home expenses (subject to limitations).

88 OPTIONS ON CLAIMING EXPENSES AGAINST COMMISSION SALES

A commission salesperson who is an employee may deduct employment expenses based on two options:

1. *Travel expenses only:* This would include auto operating costs plus Capital Cost Allowances (CCA) as well as taxi, bus, rail, air, or other transportation costs if required to travel outside of your employer's metropolitan place of business; also meals and tips, if you are away 12 hours or more. What's important about this option is that expenses may exceed commissions earned and offset other income in the year.

2. *Salesperson's expenses:* Advertising, promotion, entertainment, auto and travel expenses, as well as certain home-office expenses are claimable. But note, under this option, expenses may not exceed commissions earned, with the exception of CCA and interest on the vehicle.

89 ALLOWABLE EXPENSES FOR EMPLOYEES WHO EARN COMMISSIONS

If you negotiate contracts on behalf of your employer and receive remuneration that includes commissions in whole or in part, you may be able to deduct the same expenses noted for employees in Tip #87 above, plus:

- income tax preparation fees
- advertising and promotion costs
- entertainment and meal expenses for your clients (50% of actual expenses), provided receipts and reasons for meetings are documented
- meals (subject to 50% rule) and lodging if away for at least 12 hours
- licence and bonding costs
- insurance costs, including liability insurance
- medical underwriting fees
- leasing costs for computers, cellular phones, faxes and other electronic equipment
- cost of courses to maintain, upgrade or update your skills.

🟊 90 MOTOR VEHICLE EXPENSES OF EMPLOYEES

An employee will generally be allowed to claim motor vehicle expenses and/or travelling expenses if all of the following conditions are met:

- s/he is normally required to work away from the employer's place of business
- s/he is required to pay the motor vehicle expenses
- s/he did not receive a "non-taxable allowance" from the employer (see Tip #75)
- Form T2200 "Declaration of Employment Conditions" is filed.

Again, have the employer sign the T2200 which must be done before any claim for employment expenses can be made. Expenses that can be claimed must be supported by a distance log that charts both business and personal travel. The actual expenses claimed will be prorated based on business travel over total distance travelled. They include the following operating costs:

- gas and oil
- maintenance and repairs
- licence and insurance

- parking (usually claimed in full) and car washes (usually prorated to business/personal use);

as well as the following fixed costs:

- *interest on car loan* (maximum $8.33 a day for new loans negotiated in 1997; for loans negotiated in the period from September 1, 1989 to December 31, 1996 this amount is $10.00 a day; from June 18, 1987 to August 31, 1989 the amount was $250 a month)
- *leasing costs* (claim a maximum of $550 a month plus PST/GST for new leases negotiated in 1997; from September 1, 1989 to December 31, 1996 this amount was $650 a month plus taxes; from June 18, 1987 to August 31, 1989 the amount was $600 a month)
- *CCA on vehicle* (this is based on a maximum value of $25,000 plus taxes for new acquisitions in 1997; this was previously $24,000 plus taxes from January 1991 to December 31, 1996; from June 18, 1987 to August 31, 1989 this amount was $20,000; until the end of 1990, the amount was $24,000 without taxes).

91 DEDUCT HOME WORKSPACE EXPENSES

Home workspace expenses are claimable only if the workspace is mainly where you do your work, or you use the workspace only to earn employment income and on a regular and continuous basis for meeting clients.

	Claimable	*Not Claimable*
Salaried Employees:	1. rent	1. CCA on home
	2. utilities	2. property taxes
	3. cleaning materials	3. insurance payments
	4. minor office repairs	4. interest on mortgage
Salary and Commission:	1. 1 to 4 above	1. CCA on home
	2. property taxes	2. interest on mortgage
	3. insurance	

Expenses for workspace in the home must be allocated for employment/personal use through square footage measurement. If the space is 250 square feet and total home space is 1,500 square feet, the percentage of expenses allowed is 17%. It's a good idea to prepare a sketch of the home workspace area and how this compares to the rest of the living space in the home, in case of audit.

Home workspace expenses may not be claimed if the amounts will exceed net employment income after all other expenses are claimed. If, for example, the employee earned $12,000, other expenses were $5,000 and allowable home workspace expenses were $3,000, the full amount of allowable home workspace expenses are claimable. However, if net employment income before calculating home workspace expenses in this case was $2,000, the taxpayer must carry forward $1,000 of the workspace expenses to next year.

92 EXPENSIVE LEGAL FEES MAY BE TAX DEDUCTIBLE

It is usually a difficult and unfortunate event that causes an employee to hire a lawyer to defend his or her rights to income sources or against client grievances.

Certain legal fees are tax deductible:

1. Legal expenses incurred after 1985 to collect or establish a right to a retiring allowance or pension benefits, less any awards for costs, and amounts rolled over to an RRSP.
2. Legal expenses incurred to collect salary or wages owed to the employee by the employer.
3. Legal expenses incurred by employees who sell or negotiate contracts for events that are a normal risk of earning income from employment.
4. Legal expenses incurred to enforce payment of maintenance amounts previously established in a Family Court.
5. Legal expenses paid for assistance in filing an objection or appeal of tax, interest or penalties assessed under the Income Tax Act, a decision under the EI Commission or CPP.
6. Legal fees incurred for the purpose of gaining or producing income from business or property, including your investments.

The following legal fees are *not* tax deductible:

1. Legal expenses incurred for costs in obtaining a divorce or separation agreement.
2. Legal expenses for outlays of a capital nature (add to capital cost).
3. Legal expenses incurred for advice in preparing a tax return unless this is in connection with earning income from business or property, or selling property or negotiating contracts.
4. Legal expenses incurred to protect a real estate licence to earn commissions.
5. Legal fees attributable to an automobile accident that occurred while the vehicle was used for personal purposes.

93 SPECIAL DEDUCTIONS FOR LONG-DISTANCE TRUCK DRIVERS

Those who regularly travel away from their home terminals can deduct the costs of meals and lodging to a maximum of three meals each day; one after every four hours from checkout time. Two methods of claiming expenses are available:

(a) *Detailed:* You must keep a record book itemizing expenses and their receipts. Then claim the actual amounts paid as expenses on the tax return.

(b) *Simplified:* You must keep a detailed list of trips. Then claim $11.00 for each meal. (This "per meal" rate is subject to change but was set at $11.00 at time of writing.) There is a maximum of 3 meals in a 24-hour period, that begins at checkout time. If you travel scheduled runs of 10 hours or less, only one meal claim is allowed for lunch.

Make the claim on Revenue Canada's Form TL2 "Claim for Board and Lodging," and don't forget to claim also a GST/HST rebate for these tax-deductible expenses. The claim for meals is subject to a 50% restriction after February 21, 1994.

94 THE CLERIC'S RESIDENCE ALLOWANCE

A member of the clergy who is a regular minister of a religious denomination and in charge of a diocese, parish or congregation, or engaged exclusively in full-time administrative service by appointment of a religious order or religious denomination, can deduct an amount equal to the value of the residence or other living accommodation occupied by him or her in the course of the office or employment, to the extent that such value is included in computing income for the year. The deduction can be computed based on rent paid or the fair rental value of the residence. However, the deduction may not exceed income earned from employment.

95 ALLOWABLE MUSICAL INSTRUMENT COSTS

If you are an employed musician, check out these tax deductible items on your instruments:

- maintenance and repairs
- rental fees
- insurance costs
- CCA on the instrument.

All expenses are limited to the amount of income earned from your employment as a musician. Recover any GST/HST paid by filing Form GST/HST-370. (See line 457 on the tax return.)

96 ALLOWABLE EXPENSES OF EMPLOYED ARTISTS

Employed actors, artists, dancers, singers, musicians and writers enjoy special tax deductions for the following supplies used up in the performance of their duties:

- supplies used up (ballet shoes, body suits, chisels, paper, computer supplies)
- workspace in the home
- motor vehicle or travelling expenses.

Claim the lesser of actual expenses incurred, $1,000 and 20% of employment income from artistic activities. The claim is further reduced by any allowable musical instrument costs or CCA and interest on vehicle claimed elsewhere on return.

Note: Motor vehicle and travelling expenses as well as musical instrument costs can be claimed separately on Form T777 to escape the $1,000 or "20% of income from employment" restriction.

97 ELIGIBLE EXPENSES FOR GST/HST REBATE PURPOSES

A portion of the GST/HST you paid on your tax-deductible employment expenses are claimable on line 457 of the tax return as a credit against Total Taxes Payable. You can apply to receive this rebate for the following eligible expenses, by completing form GST/HST 370:

- accounting and legal fees
- office expenses
- travelling expenses
- entertainment expenses
- meals and lodging
- motor vehicle expenses, excluding interest, licence, or insurance
- leasing costs

- parking costs
- miscellaneous supplies (maps, pens, pencils, etc.)
- membership fees in professional organizations
- CCA on motor vehicles, aircraft and musical instruments.*

* Acquired after 1990 and for which GST/HST was paid. For 1997, those tax payers who lived in Nova Scotia, New Brunswick or Newfoundland were also subject to the HST effective April, 1997.

98 INELIGIBLE EXPENSES FOR GST/HST REBATE PURPOSES

- items not deducted on the income tax return
- CCA for any assets except those listed above
- supplies acquired from someone who is not a GST/HST registrant
- expenses incurred outside Canada (i.e., gas purchased in the U.S.)
- zero-rated supplies such as basic groceries, exported goods
- exempt supplies such as insurance premiums, mortgage interest, licence, insurance, interest and registration fees for autos, most educational services.

The GST/HST rebate is one of the most missed rebates on the tax return since its introduction in 1991. If you claimed employment expenses on line 229 and missed this rebate, file an adjustment to your return with form GST/HST-370 to receive a rebate on your tax-deductible expenditures. GST/HST rebates on operating expenses are reported on Line 104 as income in the year received; GST/HST rebates on capital assets will reduce claims for CCA.

99 BE ON THE LOOKOUT FOR SUBCONTRACTING OPPORTUNITIES

When you negotiate your next employment contract, ask yourself whether there are any barriers to providing additional services to others on a subcontracting basis. A radio disc jockey, for example, might be paid a salary to host a particular show, but might negotiate a contract independently to provide a series of special broadcasts or commercials to unrelated third parties. Will his contract of employment prohibit him from earning extra income outside of the employer's place of business?

Artists and writers often have the opportunity to be both employed and self-employed. If you are a typesetter, is there an opportunity for you to provide typesetting services to others after hours on a subcontracting basis?

Always be on the lookout for subcontracting opportunities. It's a great way to make extra money and create a series of legitimate tax deductions available to the self-employed, provided you are not prohibited by your contract of employment from doing so.

100 CLEARLY ESTABLISH THE NATURE OF YOUR WORK RELATIONSHIPS

Revenue Canada will frown on transactions that are clearly employer–employee in nature but reported as subcontracting for the potential tax benefits.

You must establish that you are truly an independent contractor, and not connected to the employer through a "master–servant" relationship, by meeting several "tests," including the following:

- you have control over where you work and how the work is done
- the work is not an integral part of the employer's business
- you bear the risk of loss and have the opportunity and right to the profits of your activities.

You can also prove your activities are independent by showing that you are providing services to a number of different individuals or companies, and that you have made your own investment in capital assets of your subcontracting enterprise.

As a subcontractor, you will file an income and expense statement to report your net profits to Revenue Canada.

CHAPTER 6

MAXIMIZE WRITE-OFFS FOR HOME-BASED BUSINESS

Do you know...

* *You can save time and money by audit-proofing your affairs...*
* *A separate business bank account and telephone line can reap tax savings...*
* *It makes "cents" to pay your family members for work done in your business...*
* *Separate tax treatment is given to operating expenses and capital expenses...*
* *Keep an Auto Log and formal records for all business transactions...*
* *A Daily Journal of business activities can help you prove reasonable expectation of profit in your start-up business...*

After 15 years of dedication to her company, Ellen, a senior executive, found herself unemployed —- the result of a corporate restructuring. There were two ways to look at this event: as a failure, or as an opportunity.

Ellen chose the latter. She opened a home-based consulting business, counselling other businesses in her field of expertise: marketing and communications.

The start was tough, but soon her appointments multiplied and the red ink on her journals turned black.

Ellen knew her silent partner, Revenue Canada, would soon be looking for its share of her profits...and she wanted to arrange her affairs so as to pay the least amount legally possible, especially since the March 6, 1996 federal budget announced that 800 new tax auditors would be hired to confirm that unincorporated small business owners, like Ellen, are in fact following the letter of the law.

101 UNDERSTAND THE ONUS OF PROOF

One of the primary differences in status between a self-employed person and an employee is the "self-assessment" that is required to report taxes owing. That is, a self-employed person must keep books and records to justify income, expenses and capital acquisitions reported of the return. Revenue Canada will normally request verification more frequently if you are self-employed. Will you be prepared to prove the figures you have used?

Always ensure the amounts you claim are supported by invoices, receipts, auto and home office logs, and reasons why the expenditures were made. Revenue Canada states that to be deductible, your expenses must be reasonable and incurred to earn business income. There must be a profit motive. That is, the write-offs you make on your return cannot be the result of a hobby, with no expectation of profits in the future. And the onus of proof of every figure on your tax return rests with you—even if you are not the one who prepared the return. If you meet all these criteria, go forth and claim all the deductions you are entitled to.

102 JUSTIFY THE REASONABLENESS OF YOUR AFFAIRS

For self-employed persons, deductible expenditures are not itemized in the Income Tax Act as they are for employees. Rather, the more "grey" application of rules exists under a general limitation in Section 18 (1) of the Act, provided a profit motive exists. That is, an outlay or expense will generally be deductible if it was incurred to earn income from business or property and if it was reasonable under the circumstances.

How can you justify reasonableness? First there is a market test. For example, paying your spouse or child much more money than you would to a stranger doing the same work, for example, would be considered unreasonable. Next, remember that a separate allocation must be made for operational expenses (those used up in the business) and capital expenses (those pertaining to assets with a useful life of more than one year).

To justify the size of business losses that are deductible against other income of the year, especially in start-up years, keep a daily business journal. In it record all business activities, whether or not they lead directly to income. Be prepared to show how networking, sourcing, and other activities eventually bear fruit.

Finally, have a focused long-term plan for your business. In that way you can show Revenue Canada that your business is a bona fide concern with future income potential, rather than just a hobby.

103 PLAN YOUR BUSINESS YEAR END CAREFULLY

New in '97

In the first year of an unincorporated small business, you can choose any time within a 12-month period to end your fiscal year...however, recent tax changes may cause you to conform to a calendar year end.

Under previous rules, a tax deferral would result if you planned your fiscal year end carefully. For example, Ellen started her business in May of 1997, one month after her employment ended. If Ellen chose a January 31 year end, she could defer reporting her business income until the next tax year, thereby deferring any tax bill.

Or, if her start-up costs exceeded her income in the first six months, Ellen could choose to end her fiscal year in October. The resulting loss from her proprietorship would offset her employment income earned during the first four months of the year. This loss application would put Ellen in a position to receive certain refundable tax credits from both the federal and provincial governments.

Unfortunately, the government has moved to put an end to tax deferrals by business people who choose to defer paying tax by selecting a non-calendar year end. An automatic "default" to a common year ending December 31 has been adopted, except in special cases. New businesses that started after 1994 will generally conform to the December 31 calendar year end. However, if there is a valid business reason to keep a non-calendar year end, Ellen may formally elect to do so, when she files her tax return, but this option may come at a price:

Should she elect to defer her year end to January 31, 1998, she will be required to compute an "additional income inclusion" for the period February 1, 1998 to December 31, 1998, on her 1998 tax return. This income inclusion is based on income earned in the off-calendar fiscal period that ended in 1998. Unfortunately, there will be no reserve or relieving provision to shelter the burden of reporting more than 12 months of income in 1998. In this situation, Ellen should see a tax professional to calculate the benefits of the tax deferral and compare it to the potential liability under the Alternative Method calculations when she files her 1997 tax return.

Most businesses in existence on December 31, 1994, with off-calendar year ends, were required to calculate income for the period ending December 31, 1995 and maintain a calendar year end thereafter. Provided these businesses were operating on December 31, 1994, a transitional reserve provision, in effect for a 10-year period, was introduced to soften the blow of the additional income inclusion resulting from these new "common year end rules." In the 1995 tax year, 95% of the additional income from the qualifying period ending December 31, 1995 could be sheltered from tax. In 1996, 85% could be sheltered, and in 1997, the reserve will be a maximum of 75% of the 1995 stub period income.

Because of these complexities, choosing a fiscal year end has important tax consequences; therefore, it is important to consult with your tax professional for the best fiscal year end strategies for your new venture.

104 UNDERSTAND THE DEFINITION OF BUSINESS INCOME

When you earn income, it can fall under several different categories, with different tax consequences. Employees, for example, generally report their income from employment: on Line 101 of the return. Investors will have different tax consequences, as discussed in Chapters 7 and 8 of this book.

An unincorporated small business owner is taxed personally on gross profits, less expenses incurred to earn income. The net profit is added to other personal income of the year in full, while net losses can be used to offset other income of the year. This is relatively straight forward.

However, you should know that the investment in a business can also have capital gains consequences. For example, if you sell an income-producing asset for more than its original cost, a capital gain will be calculated, and 75% of the resulting profit will be added to income.

In addition, an isolated transaction can be considered to be "an adventure or concern in the nature of trade," which is treated like business income. This could happen when you sell a piece of real estate, if Revenue Canada takes the stand that you are "carrying out a business" in making that transaction.

This is important because a "capital gain," which could occur when you dispose of an income-producing asset, is subject to income inclusion at 75%, while net business income is fully reportable. The difference to your pocketbook can be thousands of dollars.

There are also implications regarding the valuation of inventory. In the case of an adventure or concern in the nature of trade, for example, inventory write-downs must be postponed until disposition.

Income resulting from a capital disposition, as well as income from investment property, is calculated on a calendar-year basis.

105 KNOW THAT SOME EXPENDITURES ARE ONLY PARTIALLY DEDUCTIBLE

As mentioned earlier, eligible expenses of a business fall under more general rules than those of employment or property, which are specifically laid out in the Income Tax Act.

In order for a business expense to be deductible, it must be incurred to earn income from the business, which has a reasonable expectation of profit over a period of time. The expenses themselves must be reasonable, and not capital in nature; that is, they must be used up in the operation of the business, and usually have a useful life of less than a year. There must be an allowance for personal use and consumption of business expenditures that have otherwise been written off as a business expense.

Capital expenses — those made to acquire an asset with a useful and enduring life of more than a year — cannot be deducted as expenses in full, but rather are subject to declining balance rates, based on specific asset classifications, that have been pre-determined by Revenue Canada. Capital Cost Allowance (CCA) is then deducted as an expense at the taxpayer's option.

Therefore, to file a tax return for a small business, it is necessary to separate operating expenses from capital expenditures.

106 ALWAYS PRORATE FOR PERSONAL USE COMPONENTS

A good way to avoid problems during a tax audit is always to allocate a personal use component to expenses that are paid by the business, but are used in a personal setting.

A cosmetics salesperson, for example, might write off all the expenses of make-up and skin care products that she uses for resale. But if she fails to add back into income, a reasonable amount for personal consumption, she can expect trouble from Revenue Canada's auditors, unless she can prove she never uses any of the products herself.

Or a masonry contractor, who ships a portion of interlocking bricks to his new home, and a portion to his client's worksite, should allocate the personal use portion of the expenses, or write off only the portion of the expense that pertained to his client. *It is important to note that the construction industry has been targeted by Revenue Canada for special tax reporting after 1995. Revenue Canada will want to know, on a formal basis, what payments are made to subcontractors in construction, alteration, repair or removal of any structure, and that all income and expenses are documented.*

Similar adjustments must be made by those who run clothing stores, grocery stores, farms, fishing enterprises and the like. In addition, costs of using capital assets that have both a personal and business usage — example, a car or your home office — must reflect reductions for personal use. Expect to be asked for the personal use allocation during an audit.

107 AUDIT-PROOF YOUR AFFAIRS TO AVOID EXPENSIVE FINES

New in '97

Did you hear the one about the businessman who was fined for tax evasion? It appears again and again in newspapers and other media...certain Canadians will attempt to evade taxes by overstating deductions, understating income, or by attempting to transfer income offshore.

In October of 1996, a businessman was fined $500,000 for evading more than $332,000 in federal income taxes and sentenced to 240 hours of community service — all of this for transferring over $900,000 in corporate funds to a U.S. corporation over a period of four years.

You should know that Revenue Canada has stepped up its enforcement and compliance strategies to ensure that all Canadians work within an economy where there is a level playing field competitively, and fairness to the application of tax law.

To keep yourself out of hot water with Revenue Canada, do the following:

Submit GST/HST and PST collected on time. Make your quarterly tax instalment payment, if required, on time, to reduce interest costs.

Keep all business records in the form of invoices, receipts, auto distance logs, client appointments or vouchers relating to expenditures. Keep detailed records of transactions to prove at all times that the arrangement of your affairs was for a bona fide business purpose. Be sure to keep a log of all driving distances, personal and business. These figures are needed to prorate the allowable portion of your automobile expenses. Such books and records must be kept for a minimum of six years from the end of the year in which the Notice of Assessment is received.

Certain expenses can be claimed on an unreceipted basis: coin parking, car washes, pay telephones or any other expenses incurred where it is not possible to receive a receipt. Keep a log of such expenditures.

And remember: deliberate overstatement of expenses or understatement of income is heavily penalized: gross negligence can net a penalty of 50% of taxes owing plus interest. Fraud or tax evasion can lead to penalties of up to 200% of taxes owing and/or jail sentences.

If Revenue Canada considers your business transactions to be orchestrated in such a way as to avoid, reduce or defer taxes solely or to circumvent the intent of the law, the tax man can ignore the transactions and under GAAR — the General Anti-Avoidance Rules — assess your taxes as if the transactions did not take place.

Finally, offshore income has always been taxable to Canadian residents, who must report world income in Canadian funds, on their returns. Canadians should keep a listing of their foreign holdings in excess of $100,000 from 1996 forward, as the government has introduced proposals which may require that such a list be submitted in the future.

108 ALWAYS OPEN A SEPARATE BANK ACCOUNT FOR YOUR BUSINESS

New in '97

Don't give Revenue Canada a reason to audit all of your personal banking records during a business audit, or disallow your business losses because you have muddied your business affairs with personal transactions. Open a separate business account to which your business income is deposited and against which cheques are written. Then write off in full all banking service charges as a business expense.

This year, Revenue Canada is particularly concerned about those who write off rental losses incurred in renting real estate to relatives. Make sure you know the fair rental value of similar rental spaces in your area and that you can show a reasonable expectation of profit.

109 MEASURE OUT YOUR HOME OFFICE SPACE

A home-based business can generate a fist-full of tax deductions, based on a portion of the expenses you pay for the upkeep of your home, provided certain conditions are met.

Your home-based business qualifies for a special deduction for the workspace in the home. All expenses of the home, including mortgage interest, property taxes, insurance, utilities, maintenance and repairs may be claimed, at least in part, if you are self-employed.

To qualify for the allowable deduction, the workspace must be segregated from the rest of the personal living quarters and used solely as the place from which you earn business income. The workspace is deductible only if the office is used exclusively to earn business income on a regular and continuous basis for meeting clients, customers or patients, or if it is the principal place of business of the taxpayer.

Under the second criteria, some taxpayers may have two places of business, but the home workspace must be the principal place of business. A carpenter, for example, may spend most of the time working away from the home office, to which he returns to prepare books, book appointments, prepare cost estimates, etc.

To compute the deductible portion of your home workspace expenses, allocate what percentage of the home is used for the office, on a square-footage basis, over the total living area of the home. For example, if one room (300 square feet) out of a nine-room house (3,000 square feet) is used exclusively for the office, then one-tenth of all expenses are deductible. In some enterprises, such as child care for example, a time element may also be considered if most of the house is being used in the enterprise. In such cases, prorate all home expenses not only by actual space used, but also by hours the enterprise is open.

New in '97 110 CARRY FORWARD RESTRICTED HOME WORKSPACE DEDUCTIONS

The expenses of your home workspace are subject to a special restriction: they may not be used to increase or create a loss from your business. If this happens, claim any of the available home office expenses to reduce net business income to zero; then carry the remaining expenses forward and apply them against business income next year.

Also remember that in 1996 and future tax years, income against which deductible home office expenses are compared will be computed without regard to the reserve provisions for businesses who changed their fiscal year end to December 31, 1995.

111 AVOID CCA CLAIM TO PRESERVE YOUR TAX-EXEMPT PRINCIPAL RESIDENCE

Self-employed persons may claim a capital cost allowance deduction for their depreciable assets, including a portion of the personal residence used in the home-based business. However, this is usually not wise.

If you claim CCA on your home, the business portion of any gains on the value of the property on disposition will be considered a taxable capital gain. You can preserve your tax-exempt principal residence status on the property, however, if you avoid this deduction.

112 YOU CAN CAPITALIZE INTEREST EXPENSES ON DEPRECIABLE ASSETS

The interest you pay on money borrowed to purchase an income-producing asset is usually written off in full as an operating expense. However, you have the option of "capitalizing" this expense in order to "save" more of the write-off for future years when your profits may be higher.

This election can be made for a portion or all of the interest costs. It's one of only a few ways to defer a tax deduction into the future, and a great way to minimize your losses in your start-up years when your financial institution (and Revenue Canada) might be judging performance and profitability.

113 ESTABLISH A SEPARATE TELEPHONE LINE

To ensure you receive a tax deduction for your telephone or other communications costs, always install a separate business line. If you do not have one, generally only business-related long-distance calls will be tax deductible. Cellular air time and fax and modem long distance costs will also be deductible.

114 PAY YOUR SPOUSE OR CHILDREN FOR WORKING IN YOUR BUSINESS

A great way to split income legally is to pay your family members for work done in your business. Provided that the work was necessary, was actually done, and for a fee you would normally pay a stranger, the expense will be deductible to you, and reportable as income by your spouse or child. Prove your claim by having your family members fill in time cards or sign employment contracts with the company. It is important to pay the money to them from company funds, and to issue appropriate T4 Slips, where necessary.

The spouse or child will also be able to make RRSP contributions based on the income earned out of your business. In the case of the spouse, skillfully planning the RRSP contributions could help create a Spousal Amount on your tax return.

🏵115 WRITE OFF ALL EXPENSES FOR YOUR BUSINESS VEHICLE

New in '97

Your car, truck or van may become an asset of the business, costs for which are tax deductible when you acquire that vehicle for business purposes. You can either transfer a personal vehicle to your business at its Fair Market Value, or you can buy or lease another vehicle used primarily in the business. You would claim the "cost of addition" on your Capital Cost Allowance schedule if you transferred an existing vehicle or acquired a separate vehicle for the business.

Capital cost allowance is a method of depreciation used in tax calculations. In the year you acquire a capital asset, such as a car, only one-half of the normal depreciation rate is claimable. For a passenger vehicle, the normal depreciation rate is 30% in Class 10. If you acquire a passenger vehicle that is considered to be a "luxury vehicle" — that is one with a value greater than $24,000 (plus PST/GST) before 1997, or $25,000 plus taxes in 1997, it is placed in Class 10.1 and subject to several restrictions.

First, the depreciable capital cost is limited to $24,000 or $25,000 (plus PST/GST), even if you paid much more for a luxury car. Interest expenses are restricted to $10 per day, on loans in place between September 1, 1989 and the end of 1996. For new loans taken in 1997, this amount is $8.33 a day. And, if you leased your car in the period between September 1, 1989 and December 31, 1996, tax-deductible leasing costs may not exceed $650 per month (plus PST/GST). Deductible costs of new leases negotiated after 1996 decrease to $550 a month. However, these restrictions can be avoided if your vehicle is engaged primarily (90% of the time or more) in transporting goods, equipment or passengers.

Don't forget to claim other operating expenses, such as gas and oil, maintenance and repairs, insurance, licence fees and car club membership fees. Parking expenses are usually claimable in full, while all other operating expenses must be prorated to their business/personal usage based on distance driven for each.

116 AVOID TAX ON FREQUENT FLYER POINTS

Many businesses are now using frequent flyer points resulting from business credit card usage and legitimately deductible expense charges on these cards. No tax consequence arises from the use of such frequent flyer points if the resulting trip was for business purposes and there was no personal use component (i.e., a spouse's accompanying trip).

Any personal component of trips taken from points accumulated through tax-deductible expenditures is added into income through a "personal use adjustment" on the business income and expense statement at fair market value. The onus to report this is on the businessperson who is deducting the expenses upon which the points were accumulated.

In short, the frequent flyer benefits themselves become credits to the business, which, if used for business, have no tax consequence.

New in '97 117 CERTAIN FINES AND PENALTIES ARE TAX DEDUCTIBLE

While most parking tickets and speeding fines are not deductible at all, there are instances when fines and penalties can be deducted as legitimate business expenses; for example, when the fine or penalty can be shown to have been laid out for the purpose of earning income, or where incurring the type of fine or penalty is a normal risk of carrying on the business, and even though due care is exercised, the violation was inevitable and beyond the control of the taxpayer and his or her employees.

Specifically non-deductible are penalties imposed for default in payment of excise and federal sales tax, penalties paid for late or deficient payments of the Goods and Services Tax* or provincial sales taxes, penalties imposed under tax, customs, corporations acts or other legislation for failure to maintain books and records, fines levied by provincial law societies, accounting institutes, colleges of physicians

---

*Note: The 6% penalty on GST delinquency can be avoided through voluntary compliance.

and stock exchanges or other governing bodies, or fines or penalties for participating in illegal activities.

The following items, however, are legitimate tax deductions:

1. Interest paid on late or deficient GST, sales tax or excise tax that relates to a business or property;
2. Penalties imposed for default in payment of property or business taxes levied by a municipality, provided the taxes themselves are deductible;
3. Penalties imposed by trade organizations with common business interests, such as trade associations or farmers' associations;
4. Penalties for failure to fulfill obligations under private contracts (i.e., failure to complete a contract on schedule);
5. Penalty or bonus payable because of the pre-maturity repayment of the principal of an outstanding debt obligation. Such amounts are considered to be "prepaid interest" and therefore deductible.

Mortgage Penalties: A mortgage penalty will generally not be deductible unless the penalty is incurred in the course of carrying on a business (i.e., trading in mortgages) or in connection with a revenue property. However, a mortgage prepayment penalty for the purpose of making a capital disposition is considered to be a cost of disposition and so can be added to the taxpayer's adjusted cost base in determining the amount of capital gain or loss. Such an amount may also qualify as a moving expense. A penalty or bonus paid on repayment of a mortgage before maturity is deductible as interest, to a maximum of the interest that would otherwise have been payable for the year.

✦ New in '97 118 CHARITABLE DONATIONS MAY BE TAX DEDUCTIBLE

Charitable giving usually qualifies for a two-tiered non-refundable tax credit on the individual income tax return. On the first $200, a 17% federal credit is allowed; any amount over $200 qualifies at an increased rate of 29%. These donations are usually grouped on one spouse's return to maximize the 29% increased credit, or can be saved and carried forward to make one large claim in a five-year period. For 1996, donations of up to 50% of your net income could be claimed as a tax credit, while in 1997 and future years, up to 75% of your net income may be donated. Special provisions also exist to give extra tax benefits to those who donate publicly traded securities after February 18, 1997 and other capital property.

If you are in business for yourself, however, you might be able to claim certain charitable receipts as a promotional expense, provided that you can show that the expense was incurred to earn income from your business, either through promoting your company name or business services. With the new rule changes, carefully compute which provision gives you the best tax advantage.

119 WRITE OFF YOUR BUSINESS LOSS AGAINST INCOME OF OTHER YEARS

When your proprietorship incurs a loss, that loss is deductible against other income of the year. If you have no other income, or the loss is substantial, so that it exceeds your net income, you may carry back specified excess losses to offset income in the previous three tax years, or carry the losses forward to offset income for seven years in the future (ten in the case of farmers).

This is an excellent way to reach back (or forward) to recover taxes paid, so keep meticulous records every year of such events. However, be aware that taxpayers who previously claimed a reserve under the 1995 fiscal year end rules may find that tax deductible current year losses may be impacted by the reserve provisions and vice versa. It may be best to check with your tax professional in that case, as the computations are complicated.

7

HOW TO PRODUCE INCOME FROM YOUR INVESTMENTS

Do you know...

* *You can save up to 50% or more of your contributions to an RRSP in tax savings...*
* *You can use RRSP contribution room to reduce tax on retiring allowances...*
* *You can reduce your overall tax burden by diversifying your investments held in non-registered accounts...*
* *You can transfer dividends earned in non-registered investments between spouses...*
* *You can offset capital gains of the year with current or prior year capital losses...*

For some unfortunate investors in Bre-X and other shares, proper application of tax provisions will have a critical impact on the after-tax results of investment results. Others, who have had a joy ride in the marketplace, will want to maximize RRSP contributions, which have been capped at $13,500 per year until 2003, and shelter the rest of their capital from tax, if possible. Yet others, particularly seniors who turn 69 during the year (69, 70 or 71 in 1997) face major investment decisions as they are required to mature their RRSP deposits.

The name of the game is tax sheltering and deferral in these years of peak tax rates in Canada. To come out a winner, you may need the help of a sharp tax advisor, an experienced investment planner and a lawyer who can help you prepare an intelligent estate plan for you.

✹120 USE RRSP ROOM PROVISION TO YOUR BEST ADVANTAGE

It is possible, for example, that you, like many others in Canada, are carrying forward a sizable RRSP contribution room balance from the years 1991 to the present. The question one must ask is "Why?" Why would you pay more tax than you have to? Why would you miss out on the opportunities to make tax sheltered investments?

When times are good, and you are healthy enough to produce earnings that create RRSP room, try to make the contribution. It will save you big money on your taxes — 26% to over 50% depending on your marginal tax bracket and province of residence. You might even consider taking advantage of over-contribution rules as a hedge against future cash flow problems.

There are times when taking an RRSP deduction may not be in your best tax interest. For example, if you are single and earned less than the basic personal amount, you won't be taxable. But, perhaps you have unused RRSP contribution room of $5,000. Should you make a contribution?

The answer is probably yes. You should make the RRSP contribution, but you may choose to claim the actual deduction in another year when you need it to reduce taxable income. In other words, you will now have an "undeducted RRSP contribution balance" for use in future years. When should you forego the RRSP contribution? Perhaps when you don't need the deduction to reduce taxable income and you have other non-deductible debt, such as personal credit card balances. Speak to your financial planner for more direction, if needed.

To maximize your opportunities under tax-sheltered registered retirement plans, you must first know what income sources qualify for RRSP earned income (described below). Then make a point of contributing to an RRSP and deducting the contribution in a year when you can get the biggest tax bang for your buck. This will generally be when taxable income is at a high marginal tax rate. Remember, RRSP room can now be carried forward indefinitely into the future. Keep track of that plus all undeducted RRSP contributions.

✹121 UNDERSTAND WHAT RRSP EARNED INCOME IS

If you had the following income sources last year, you will probably have the required RRSP contribution room to allow you to make a tax-deductible RRSP contribution:

1. Salary or wages before deduction of EI (Employment Insurance)

premiums, CPP or RPP (Registered Pension Plans through employment), employee contributions to a Retirement Compensation Arrangement, or the cleric's residence deduction;

2. Income from royalties of works by an author or inventor;
3. Net income from carrying on a business where the taxpayer is actively engaged in daily operations alone or as a partner;
4. Net rental income;
5. Net research grants;
6. Supplemental unemployment insurance benefits;
7. Taxable Child Support payments or repayments included in income, (generally based on pre-May 1, 1997 agreements) or support payments received by a spouse;
8. Employee Profit Sharing Plan allocations (Box 35 of the T4PS);
9. After 1990, income received from a CPP/QPP disability benefit.

LESS:

Refunds of salary, wages, or research grants, union dues, professional dues, other employment expenses on line 229, net losses from carrying on an active business, net rental losses, alimony or child support payments deducted or repaid, and amounts included in business income on account of the disposition of eligible capital property, which represent additional negative balances in excess of recaptured deductions.

The result is "earned income." The lesser of 18% of earned income or the maximum dollar limitation (see below) is your current year's maximum RRSP contribution.

122 KNOW WHAT YOUR MAXIMUM DOLLAR LIMITATION IS

In order to contribute the maximum allowable dollar amount into your RRSP, you must earn the following:

Tax Year	Maximum Dollar Limitation	Earned Income Needed*	In Year
1991	$11,500	$63,889	1990
1992	$12,500	$69,444	1991
1993	$12,500	$69,444	1992
1994	$13,500	$75,000	1993
1995	$14,500	$80,556	1994
1996-2003	**$13,500**	**$75,000**	**1995-2002**
2004	$14,500	$80,556	2003
2005	$15,500	$86,111	2004

*This represents prior year income levels needed to contribute the maximum-dollar ceiling to an RRSP.

After 2005, maximum ceiling levels will be indexed to growth in the average industrial wage in Canada.

123 KNOW HOW MUCH RRSP CONTRIBUTION ROOM YOU HAVE

Your RRSP contribution room is based on the prior year's earned income, this year's maximum dollar limitation, and whether or not you contribute to a registered pension plan at your place of employment. If you do, your contribution room will be reduced by a "PA" or Pension Adjustment amount. You can find this figure in Box 52 of your T4 Slip, or Box 34 of a T4A of the immediately prior year.

The contributions you make to your company's registered pension plan will always be linked to your RRSP contribution room under current tax rules. In 1997 a new adjustment will be tracked that can have an affect on your 1998 RRSP contribution: Pension Adjustment Reversals (PAR) will now be available in cases where employees leave their jobs without all the pension benefits that were previously used to limit RRSP room. If this happened to you check with the Human Resources Department of your employer to determine RRSP eligibility.

In addition, any unused contribution room from prior years (starting in 1991) will increase your current room. The easiest way to find your RRSP Contribution Room for the current year is to look at last year's Notice of Assessment from Revenue Canada, but as described below, this may not be all the information required.

124 MAXIMIZE PREVIOUSLY UNUSED RRSP CONTRIBUTION ROOM

Gather the following information before making an RRSP contribution:
1. Unused contribution room since 1991 (based on 1990 earned income);
2. 18% of your earned income from the immediate prior tax year;
3. Prescribed maximum contribution dollar levels (as described above);
4. Any Pension Adjustment (PA) amount, for those who belong to a Registered Pension Plan or Deferred Profit Sharing Plan (RPP or DPSP), or for 1997 and future years, any PAR;
5. Any amounts that qualify for tax-free transfers over and above the normal limitations;

6. Actual undeducted contributions made in the current or prior year;

7. Designated amounts to be used as a repayment under the Home Buyers' Plan.

Once calculated, allowable RRSP contributions can be "topped up" in the current tax year or within 60 days of the current tax year end.

Check your Revenue Canada Notice of Assessment for your RRSP contribution room first. But if you failed to file a tax return in the past, have a pending reassessment on your tax return, or have qualifying income for tax free rollovers, (described below) the amount you can contribute to an RRSP will differ from the figure on the Notice of Assessment.

125 COMMON SOURCES ELIGIBLE FOR TAX-FREE TRANSFERS TO AN RRSP

Make plans to defer taxes by "rolling over" or contributing the following sources of income to an RRSP:

1. Retiring Allowances, for service after 1988 and before 1996, a single limit of $2,000 per year of employment may be contributed. For employment before 1989, the limit is $2,000 for each year of employment plus $1,500 for each year in which none of the employer contributions to a company pension plan is vested in the taxpayer. (This may happen in periods of temporary or short-term employment.) Note that for service after 1995, the government has abolished the $2,000 per-year-of-service tax deferral completely. This will leave your retiring allowances paid for post-1995 service subject to income inclusion in the year received, in full. Try to negotiate the receipt of the retiring allowance over two tax years, if possible, to minimize tax in those cases, or negotiate the continuation of tax free or taxable benefits after you retire.

2. Refund of Premiums received on death of a spouse or common-law spouse, or in some cases, a supporting individual.

3. Lump-Sum Payments out of non-registered foreign pension plans for services performed while not a resident of Canada.

4. RRSP commutation payments directly transferred to another RRSP.

5. Excess amounts from a RRIF directly transferred to the RRSP.

126 USE SPOUSAL RRSPS TO YOUR MAXIMUM ADVANTAGE

A great way to reduce the taxes you'll pay in later years, and to maximize refundable tax credits in the future is to plan now to split income from RRSP accumulations between spouses. Each spouse may contribute to an RRSP based on his/her own RRSP contribution room, which was built with actively earned income sources.

In addition, though, it is possible for a high-income earner to make an RRSP contribution for a spouse who may not have earned income — perhaps during child-bearing years. In such cases, a portion of or all of the RRSP contribution may be made to an RRSP in the name of the lower earner, with the added benefit that the higher earner can still take the tax deduction. This is called making a "Spousal RRSP" contribution.

Later, in retirement, or in a year when the spouse otherwise has a lower income, withdrawals from the RRSP will be taxed in that lower-income earner's hands. However there is one catch. That is, that the RRSP accumulations cannot be touched until three years from the last spousal RRSP contribution. Otherwise, earlier withdrawals will be taxed in the hands of the higher-income earner and that would likely defeat the whole idea behind the RRSP Spousal Plan.

This planning is especially important in light of the proposed new Seniors Benefit on the horizon for the years 2001 and beyond. Spousal RRSP withdrawals also create capital that is attributed to the lower-income earner, with the result that subsequent investment earnings from these amounts will be taxed in that lower earner's hands. Therefore the act of depositing money into a Spousal RRSP will provide a multitude of income-splitting opportunities — all within the framework of the law — in the future.

127 KNOW THE DIFFERENCE BETWEEN EFFECTIVE AND MARGINAL TAX RATES

By understanding the difference between your marginal tax rate and your effective tax rate, you can increase your after tax dollar by choosing your investments wisely.

Your effective tax rate is the rate of tax you end up paying on your taxable income for the year. Your marginal tax rate is the amount of tax you pay on the next dollar you earn.

By knowing a bit more about your effective and marginal tax rates you will be able to work with your financial planner in maximizing after-tax investment return through income diversification. This is also a great way to spread out risk.

✦128 KNOW YOUR MARGINAL TAX RATE

Certain investment yields are taxed more advantageously than others, as the chart below describes:

Marginal Tax Rate: 1992 to 1997
(Approximate Federal and Provincial Rates)
(Check with your own Tax Advisor for Exact Computations in your Province of Residence)

Taxable Income	$100 Interest	$100 Dividends	$100 Excess Capital Gains*
$25,000	27%	8%	20%
$39,000	42%	27%	31%
$75,000	50%	34%	37%

*Capital Gain unsheltered by the Capital Gains Deduction.

Investors earning dividends and capital gains outside of an RRSP still enjoy lower marginal tax rates on their investments than those with interest income. Marginal tax rates will vary from province to province with different income sources and within age groups, so check yours out with your tax advisor.

129 DIVERSIFY YOUR INVESTMENT PORTFOLIO FOR MAXIMUM AFTER TAX EARNINGS

Individuals with taxable incomes in the $35,000 range may be surprised to know that interest earnings, such as those reaped from investments in Canada Savings Bonds or term certificates, are taxed at a marginal tax rate of approximately 40%. That is, about 40 cents out of every dollar earned on that investment goes back to the federal and provincial governments by way of taxes.

The same is true of the taxation of RRSP or RRIF withdrawals. Because both principal and earnings must be added to income in full, it is particularly important to plan around marginal tax brackets for different income "benchmarks."

There is much you can do to keep taxes out of the hands of the government. For example, you can generate only enough earnings, in some cases, to keep a taxpayer in the family under the Personal Tax Credit Amounts. For example, if one spouse has little or no income, while the other is in a high tax bracket, withdrawals up to the Basic Personal Amount ($6,456 for those under 65 or $9,938 for those age 65 or more) will be received on a tax free basis. (However, the higher figure will lose the Spousal Amount; yet there may be other gains under medical expense provisions.)

Alternatively, if one spouse is in a 50% bracket and the other in a 27% bracket, it will generally make sense to earn interest income or take RRSP or RRIF withdrawals in the lower earner's hands first. The higher earner should continue to shelter earnings within registered plans as long as possible, and attempt to earn investment income in non-registered plans in the form of dividends or capital gains. Remember that tax on capital gains will only be paid on disposition of the asset — increases in the value of the assets will not be taxed before then. This gives you a significant tax deferral opportunity — if you are comfortable with the inherent risks attached to some of these assets.

The structure of our tax rates provides a compelling reason for some taxpayers to diversify their investment portfolio. It pays to speak to tax and investment advisors about your options.

130 MAXIMIZE BOTH INCOME AND CAPITAL YIELDS

When you invest in an income-producing asset, you usually have two opportunities to make money: through the earnings of the investment (interest, dividends, rental income, business income) or through the capital appreciation of the asset itself (i.e., when you sell the asset, hopefully for more money than it cost to acquire it).

Most common "debt obligations" — Canada Savings Bonds, Guaranteed Investment Certificates, term deposits — do not provide an opportunity for capital appreciation. Interest is earned in return for the use of your money over a period of time. But does the interest rate exceed the inflation rate? And pay attention to the tax bite: interest accruals must be reported annually, meaning that Revenue Canada gets its revenue on the earnings before you do; as well, interest earnings are included in income in full, on top of all other income of the year. So, there is both tax and inflation risk.

T-Bills may afford you the opportunity for both interest earnings and capital appreciation. However, shares or mutual fund investments trading on the stock market or investments in a private Canadian corporation may yield "dividends," as well as capital appreciation — or depreciation. Publicly traded securities, or other privately held properties can accumulate value without attracting tax and this may give you some tax advantages now.

For this reason the proper "asset mix" will take into account most forms of investment risk and tax savings opportunities. Speak to your tax and investment advisors about the right strategies for you.

✿131 UNDERSTAND THE REPORTING OF INTEREST ON CANADA SAVINGS BONDS

Volatile rates of return may cause some investors to hesitate making long-term decisions, but nonetheless, for various reasons, it is usually a good idea to consider parking some of your money in interest-bearing investments. For example, it may be convenient to purchase a Canada Savings Bond through a payroll plan at work. (Don't forget to write off your interest charges in this case.)

The easiest way to consider the reporting of Canada Savings Bonds held outside a registered plan, is to determine three things:

1. Are the bonds producing interest on a Regular or Compounding basis?
2. If Compounding, interest earned will generally be reported annually, except in three very specific Series, described below.
3. What group of bonds do they fall into?
   (a) *Series 27 — 35* (all matured): their interest was reported when received.
   (b) *Series 36 — 41* (all matured): these were to have been reported annually or at least triennially.
   (c) *Series 42 — 44:* these compounding bonds have to be reported at a minimum of every three years, but the taxpayer can choose to start reporting annually at any time and for any number of bonds. In the year reporting is changed, all previously unreported interest must be "caught up" and reported. Series 42 matured in 1997 and Series 43 must be reported on the triennial basis in 1997.
   (d) *Series 45 (1990 issues and onward):* these bonds, compounding or regular, must be reported on an annual accrual basis and a T5 slip will be issued.

132 T-BILLS CAN BE A VIABLE ALTERNATIVE INVESTMENT

Treasury Bills are issued at a discount. For tax purposes, the difference between the issue price and the value at maturity is reported as interest. If you sell before maturity, calculate the interest component as follows:

$$\text{Effective Yield} \times \frac{\text{Days Held}}{\text{Days in the Year}} \times \text{Purchase Price}$$

If you sell the bill before it matures, you may also incur a capital gain or loss. Compute this as follows: Take the proceeds of disposition less interest accrued during the period held, and reduce this figure by the adjusted cost base. The result is the capital gain or loss. For example:

1. Cost of T-Bill at discount is recorded: $15,000
   (Maturity Value is $18,000)

2. Interest earned on the T-Bill to date: $ 2,000

3. Calculation of Capital Component:
   Proceeds of Disposition: $21,000 (a)
   Adjusted Cost Base: Cost $15,000
                  Interest $ 2,000
                                     $17,000 (b)

4. Capital Gain (a – b) = $ 4,000

133 AVOID THESE COMMON ERRORS IN REPORTING INTEREST INCOME

(New in '97)

Despite being the most common investment income source, taxpayers do make errors in reporting interest earnings. For example, most taxpayers miss reporting interest payments made to them, as shown on Revenue Canada's Notice of Assessment.

Canada Savings Bond interest can be double reported if records on prior-reported earnings are not kept for compounding bonds.

Interest is always reported by the person who earned the original principal; therefore, ensure that in the case of joint accounts the interest reporting accurately reflects this.

In the year a taxpayer dies, claim interest earned to date of death only on final return. The accrued portion of triennially-reported investments that pertain to years other than the year of death, may be reported as "Rights or Things" on an elective return in the year of death. This will enable the estate to claim another set of personal tax credits, and save the tax on some or all of these earnings. All other amounts of interest earned after date of death are reported by the beneficiaries or by the estate.

134 CLAIM THE DIVIDEND TAX CREDIT AGAINST RETURNS FROM CANADIAN CAPITAL STOCK

Dividends represent the after-tax profits distributed by a corporation to its shareholders. The corporation already has paid tax on these profits, so the individual shareholder receives a dividend tax credit for the taxable dividends reported on the tax return, in order to avoid double-taxation.

The actual dividends received are "grossed up" by 25% to attain their "taxable" status. Then the dividend tax credit is calculated as 13.33% of this grossed-up taxable dividend, and used to reduce federal taxes payable.

135 TRANSFER DIVIDENDS EARNED BETWEEN SPOUSES

The dividend tax credit is useful only if there is taxable income. It can't be carried forward, so for that reason it may be of benefit for a spouse with a low income to transfer dividend income and the related dividend tax credit to the higher-income earner. This is allowable, but only if certain conditions are met.

If your spouse has little or no income, consider having this person invest monies received in their own right in dividend-producing stocks. Provided you can create or increase a Spousal Amount elsewhere on the tax return, you can transfer both the dividends and the dividend tax credit to the higher-income earner's return. Prepare your family's returns both ways to determine the best benefit.

136 CREATE A CAPITAL GAIN RATHER THAN ORDINARY INCOME

In general, a capital gain will occur when you dispose of an income-producing asset for more than it cost to acquire it (including the cost of improvements). A capital gain is reported on Schedule 3 in full. It is then reduced by current-year capital losses, if any; 75% of any remaining gains are added to income on page 1 of the T1 General. For some specific types of assets, the $500,000 Capital Gains Deduction may still be available to offset such a gain. This deduction would be taken on line 254. In addition, transfers of certain publicly traded securities after February 18, 1997 to a favourite charity could qualify for a 37.5% income inclusion.

A capital gain may also occur when there is a "deemed disposition." For example, when a person dies, it is considered that all assets are disposed of at their fair market value immediately before death. If the asset passes to you, that fair market value at the time of death is your acquisition cost.

To compute capital gains or losses, take the proceeds of disposition (which can be sales proceeds or Fair Market Value on deemed dispositions) and subtract from this the Adjusted Cost Base of the asset (which can be its original cost plus all improvements, a specific Valuation Day value, or for many of those who previously made capital gains elections, the elected value). Finally subtract from this any out-lays or expenses of the sale, such as real estate commission. The result is your capital gain or loss.

Remember that accrued values on capital assets are never taxed until disposition. This provides a method of sheltering wealth accumulations.

137 AVERAGE THE COSTS OF IDENTICAL PROPERTIES AND STOCK SPLITS

Taxpayers sometimes purchase shares of the same or identical class of the capital stock of a corporation, but at varying times. As well, they may sell such identical shares at varying times and at varying prices. Such transactions within the same group of shares requires the comput-ing of an "average cost" of the shares each time there is a purchase, in order to properly compute any future gain or loss on disposition.

To calculate average cost, determine cost of the shares in the group and divide by the total number of shares held. For shares held before 1972, special rules for valuation apply.

Note: On a stock split, the average cost is affected, but no capital gain or loss transaction occurs until the taxpayer actually disposes of some or all of the shares.

138 OFFSET CAPITAL GAINS WITH CAPITAL LOSSES

It would be great to hold only winners, but the reality is, most portfo-lios also hold a few losers. You can minimize your capital losses by realizing them in a year you sell other winners — perhaps your rental property or other stocks — if this otherwise makes sense.

Capital gains of the year can then be offset by any capital losses incurred. If you have no other capital gains in the year, allowable losses must be either carried back for use against capital gains in the previous three tax years, or carried forward indefinitely. It is generally best to carry such losses forward if you previously offset gains with the capital gains deduction.

In the year of or on the final return, it is possible to offset other income of the year with unused capital loss balances. Offset capital gains of the year first. Then, before any excess losses can be applied against *other income* of the final year, they must be reduced by previously claimed capital gains deductions. For this reason, it may be wiser to carry back excesses for use against unsheltered *capital gains,* if any, in the previous year.

❋ 139 CAPITAL GAINS ELECTIONS CAN SAVE TAX DOLLARS

The February 22, 1994 federal budget eliminated the $100,000 Capital Gains Deduction for most capital assets. This means that capital gains on disposition of assets acquired after February 22, 1994 will be added into income without the benefit of this lucrative deduction. But, if you held certain assets acquired prior to this date, you were able to elect to report accrued gains from the time of acquisition to February 22, 1994 at an amount between the adjusted cost base and the Fair Market Value at February 22, 1994. The election was made on the 1994 tax return.

In the 1995 tax year, accrued gains on the eligible capital property of businesses whose fiscal years, ending in 1995, included the February 22, 1994 date, also qualified for an election.

The offsetting Capital Gains Deduction was then applied to this deemed gain, creating a virtual tax free accounting of the assets' increased values. For most assets, these "deemed" proceeds of disposition are used as the new "Adjusted Cost Base" for future capital dispositions; for others, such as mutual funds, an "exempt gains" pool was created, to be used to reduce future gains on those assets.

It is now too late to make a late-filed election. Previously filed elections could only be amended or revoked until December 31, 1997. So that leaves us with the residual effects of this provision — an ability to reduce capital gains on previously elected assets with their new ACB, in the year the disposition actually occurs.

140 AUDIT PROOF YOUR CAPITAL ASSET VALUATIONS

You might be required to obtain a Fair Market Valuation (FMV) of capital assets you own to determine your "Proceeds of Disposition" in the following instances:
- to justify the figures used on your capital gains election
- upon transfer of capital property to another individual
- upon death of the taxpayer, which triggers a "deemed disposition" of assets
- upon immigration to or emigration from Canada
- upon change of use of assets from personal to business use or vice versa
- to calculate a principal residence exemption when a second residence is disposed of.

The onus of proof rests with the taxpayer. To justify FMV when you report such a capital disposition to Revenue Canada, document the following information meticulously:

- for publicly traded shares —- stock market quotations on date of disposition
- securities of private corporations —- business valuations by certified expert
- real estate —- newspaper listings, appraisals, land registry, property tax assessments, municipal records
- art, stamp, coin collections, newspapers —- dealers, appraisers, catalogues.

If your asset acquisition dates back to pre-1972 days, obtain valuation as of December 31, 1971 (December 22, 1971, in the case of publicly traded shares).

 141 LABOUR-SPONSORED VENTURE CAPITAL TAX CREDITS

A federal tax credit is allowed for investments in approved shares of the capital stock of a prescribed labour-sponsored venture capital corporation at any time during the year or the first 60 days of the new year. For shares acquired after March 5, 1996, the credit is 15% of the cost of the shares up to a maximum of $3,500, for a maximum credit of $525. This means that in 1997 there will only be a single calculation of the federal credit. Most of these credits on the provincial side will conform to the new rules, except in the province of Prince Edward Island, where the credit has been discontinued.

These investments are also RRSP-eligible, so the taxpayer may in fact also take an RRSP deduction for the same investment. This "triple header" tax credit makes some investors think favourably about placing some dollars into these funds. However, the terms for investment are often lengthy (in fact you will be prohibited from claiming a similar tax credit for the year of redemption or either of the new two tax years, if you don't hold the shares for at least eight years). The investments can be risky, so consider your options carefully.

 142 DEDUCT YOUR INVESTMENT EXPENSES

Revenue Canada allows taxpayers to write off their investment expenses as they are incurred, including interest on money borrowed to make the non-registered investment in the first place, but this year there are new rules for some.

Likely, your largest non-deductible interest payment is your mortgage. You can create deductible interest by starting a home-based business and writing off a portion of the interest pertaining to the home office, as previously described. Or you can actually pay off your mortgage and then remortgage and use the money for investment purposes. (Any such transaction should only be attempted after seeking professional help to compute the net benefits, based on your projected investment return, mortgage interest rate, remortgaging fees, projected asset mix held outside your RRSP/RRIF, and the marginal rate of the tax savings on the interest expense.)

Your deductible interest can be used to offset other income of the year, without limitation. This will increase your tax refund, which can be reinvested in new investments or used to pay down your debt.

Be aware that investment expenses will create or increase a CNIL (Cumulative Net Investment Loss) balance, which could reduce or eliminate the $500,000 Capital Gains Exemption for qualifying assets (Qualifying Farm Property or Small Business Corporation shares). Also remember, RRSP/RRIF Administration fees will not be deductible starting in 1996 and future years, while RESP fees and expenses will not be deductible starting in 1998. Interest expenses on registered investments are not deductible.

143 INTEREST EXPENSE DEDUCTIONS ARE LUCRATIVE — AND ENDURING

There must be potential earnings from an investment before interest charges on a loan can be considered tax-deductible. You must be able to trace the borrowed funds to a specific income-producing usage. Under previous rules deductibility of the expenses ceased if the source of the income for which interest is being paid no longer existed and the borrowed funds could not be traced to another income-producing purpose.

However, new rules are in force for investments that cease to have an income-producing purpose or have suffered a loss in value. This is important news for investors who are forced to continue to pay interest on the debt.

If the original money was used to buy an eligible property, and a portion of that money has been lost because of a decline in the value of the property, the interest paid on the portion that has been lost will continue to be tax deductible, even if the asset has been disposed of. If the taxpayer borrows money to pay off the original debt, the interest on the new loan will be deductible. For example, if you borrowed $1,000 to acquire shares that have declined to their current market value of $500, the interest will continue to be deductible on the basis of the original value, even if you sell the shares.

144 CLAIM YOUR SAFETY DEPOSIT BOX AND OTHER CARRYING CHARGES

The following "carrying charges" are deductible against other income of the year, yet are frequently missed by both taxpayers and their advisors. Look back to see if you have receipts to justify the following:

- safety deposit box fees
- accounting/record-keeping fees pertaining to investments
- Canada Savings Bonds payroll deduction fee
- insurance policy loan interest
- interest expenses for loans taken for investment purposes
- for assets held *outside* an RRSP or RRIF:
  - investment counsel fees
  - management fees
  - safe custody fees

145 NEW RULES FOR RRSP/RRIF/RESP FEES

The March 6, 1996 federal budget made an important tax change that could cause you some headaches come tax time. RRSP or RRIF administration fees are no longer tax deductible as carrying charges.

If you usually pay these fees from the assets within your RRSP, there will be no tax consequence. If you usually give your carrier a cheque for the $125 or $150 it normally costs for these services (also called trustee fees) there will be no tax write-off as in the past.

There is a tricky little provision, however, for those who pay RRSP/RRIF "management fees." These fees are usually paid for custody of your securities, maintenance of your accounting records or fees based on the value of your assets. If these amounts are paid from within the RRSP, there is no tax consequence.

However, if you pay these fees with money coming from outside your RRSP, the amounts will be considered a tax deductible RRSP contribution...which is only meaningful if you have RRSP contribution room. This also means that the payment of such fees — which can be fairly extensive in the case of wrap accounts — will be subject to the $2000 over-contribution limit. So get some professional help with this.

And here's a red flag! Payment for management fees of a RRIF must be considered a non-deductible personal expense, as any contributions into a RRIF will deregister it! So pay these fees with the assets within the plan.

Finally, the government has also moved to clarify that, effective the 1998 tax year, RESP fees paid will also be non-deductible.

146 USE ALL OF YOUR ASSETS TO CREATE INVESTMENT POSSIBILITIES

Talent and opportunity, used hand in hand, can help you create wealth quickly. For example, if you are a talented employee, consider asking your employer for a low- or no-interest loan. You'll be taxed on the difference between the rate of interest your employer charges you (which could be nil) and the current prescribed rate of interest (which is based on 90-day Treasury bill yields). At recent low interest rates this could be the benefit of the century! A repayment schedule will be required.

However, the loan can be used to help you inch closer to your financial goals. If invested in income-producing assets, the taxable benefit you are assessed on the loan (check your T4 Slip) is tax deductible as a carrying charge.

Alternatively, you may possess a life insurance policy that has built up a cash value. If you borrow against this cash value, any interest paid back to the policy becomes tax deductible if the loan is used for an income-producing property.

147 ACCOUNT FOR YOUR CNIL BALANCE TO AVOID SURPRISES

The year 1988 was the one in which CNIL was introduced — Cumulative Net Investment Losses. This is the excess of investment expenses claimed over a taxpayer's lifetime (starting with the 1988 tax year) over investment earnings reported in the same period. This provision essentially acknowledges the taxpayer's ability to deduct investment expenses such as interest and other carrying charges on an annual basis, but reduces any available Capital Gains Deduction by the amount of any CNIL balance in the year a qualifying capital disposition is reported.

After the removal of the $100,000 Capital Gains Deduction in 1994, the only taxpayers who still have to be concerned with CNIL are those who will sell Qualified Farm Property or Small Business Corporation Shares in the future.

For example, assume George Lucky borrowed $20,000 in 1988 to purchase shares in a Small Business Corporation. From 1988 to 1997, he claimed interest expenses of $8,000, and no other investment income.

 (a) He can deduct the interest expenses when they were incurred.

 (b) He has a CNIL of $8,000.

Upon sale of his shares in January of the current year he realized $40,000 on disposition of the shares. His $20,000 capital gain qualifies for the $500,000 Capital Gains Exemption. The actual deduction must first, however, be calculated by taking into account the CNIL balance of $8,000.

CHAPTER

8

CREATE WEALTH WITH YOUR PERSONAL PROPERTIES

Do you know...

* *Renting out a portion of your home can help you create wealth...*
* *You can minimize taxes paid on revenue properties...*
* *There are tax advantages if you transfer assets to children...*
* *Rental income qualifies as earned income for RRSP purposes...*
* *Profits from the sale of your principal residence are tax exempt...*

Someone once said that the biggest mistake you can make is to believe you work for someone else. Only you can build your own financial legacy through the priorities and commitments you select and decisions you make.

To lead your family to financial freedom, you will need three things:

1. A definite financial goal or vision, both in the short and long term;
2. A well-thought-out action plan to help you achieve your goals;
3. Outstanding professional resources to help you maximize your options.

A common choice in the road to financial freedom is the acquisition of one or more residences. June and Tom, for example, have secured a fine home, with a substantial mortgage to chip away at. While this seems to consume a large portion of their monthly resources, Tom and June wanted to make their money work for them, instead of the other way around. Was the purchase of the home the right decision? How can they make their current efforts pay off in the long run?

148 REVIEW THE FAMILY TAX CONSEQUENCES OF ACQUIRING REAL ESTATE

Buying a family dwelling can be a good tax planning decision, particularly if other factors — such as good price, good location, and an upward-moving market environment — all work in tandem.

Whether you own a single dwelling, duplex, condo, cottage, mobile home or other property, disposition at a value higher than original cost plus improvements will generally be taxable as a capital gain — except in the case of your principal residence. Gains accrued in your primary residence can be earned on a tax-free basis, to a maximum of one tax-free residence for a family unit.

The acquisition of second and third residences, however, may require a certain amount of planning to avoid a large tax liability upon your demise, or when you transfer or sell the property to someone else, including your family members. Remember, Revenue Canada considers a "deemed disposition" at Fair Market Value occurs immediately prior to date of death, or at a time when assets are transferred to persons other than your spouse, or when there is a change of use of an asset from business to personal use. Resulting capital gains, if any, may sometimes be deferred with special elections.

When you know and understand these rules, you can quickly turn your family investments into wealth producers...and watch market trends to make sure transfers at FMV are made at the most advantageous time from a tax point of view.

149 INVEST IN A TAX-EXEMPT PRINCIPAL RESIDENCE

Many seniors today are wealthier than their parents, for several reasons including enhanced pensions through the Canada Pension Plan, Old Age Security, company pensions and RRSPs, as well as the fact that many own, rather than rent, their own homes.

Every family unit may hold one tax-exempt principal residence at any given time in a year. That is, any gains on the disposal of a principal residence can be received tax free, provided that you have not claimed a Capital Cost Allowance (CCA) deduction on the property while you owned it, and you do not have more than one principal residence at a time.

Prior to 1982, each spouse in a family unit could own one tax-exempt principal residence. Often the husband owned the cottage and the wife the house, or vice versa. On subsequent sale of each property, the resulting gains were tax exempt.

It is therefore possible that in such cases, where two residences have been held and maintained since before 1982, each may have a "tax exempt" component. In such cases be sure to seek experienced assistance in preparing Form T2091 Designation of Principal Residence.

150 SAVE A DOWN PAYMENT FOR YOUR STARTER HOME OR COTTAGE

While saving for a new home may seem overwhelming, it's really not so difficult. To begin, get a sense of how much of a down payment you need. Then, determine how much you can save and earn to help you get there in the least possible time frame. It's possible that by filing a tax return in the most advantageous way, Revenue Canada can help you with your homebuying.

If you'd like to save $25,000 for a down payment, for example, you'll need to earn an extra $50,000 (if you're in a 50% tax bracket) to make your investment appear. You might crack this nut — with tax savings from an RRSP.

If you have RRSP contribution room, invest the tax savings you reap from your RRSP contribution in an accumulating fund that builds into a downpayment. If you qualify to contribute $12,500 to your RRSP, for example, you'll save $6,250 each year in taxes payable at the same marginal tax rate of 50%. At that rate, it will take you less than four years to save for your home or cottage ($6,250 × 4 = $25,000), if you consider there will also be investment earnings on the $6,250 you save and reinvest each year.

In order to qualify to make a $12,500 RRSP deduction, you have to earn $69,444 in the immediately preceding tax year, or have substantial RRSP Room carried forward since 1991. This could be a challenge if you make $40,000 at your job. You could take on a part-time job, rent out a portion of your current home, diversify passive investments or start a small business in order to bolster your earnings. Productivity is the key.

You and your spouse could also take a joint approach: make a list of all consumer spending that can be eliminated. Instead, invest these savings in the home or cottage fund. If you both work at a job or self-employment venture, use your spouse's after-tax earnings in their entirety to save for the project, if you can otherwise afford to do so.

Or, if you already have RRSP accumulations, tap into the benefits of the RRSP Home Buyers' Plan. . . .

151 TAP INTO THE TAX-FREE RRSP HOME BUYERS' PLAN

When it was first introduced, the RRSP Home Buyers' Plan enabled a buyer to withdraw up to $20,000 in the RRSP on a tax-free basis to acquire a qualifying home in the period February 26, 1992 to March 1, 1993. This provision was extended to allow "excluded withdrawals" to be made in the period December 2, 1992 to March 1, 1994. Under these old rules no tax-deductible RRSP contribution could be made in the year in which a home buyer's withdrawal was made.

New rules introduced with the February 22, 1994 budget extended the plan again — this time for first-time home buyers only. These are people who have not owned a principal residence in the five calendar years before making a withdrawal from their RRSP.

Contributions made within the 90 days of a home buyer's withdrawal will not be deductible unless a balance equal to or greater than the withdrawal remains in the RRSP.

Any amounts withdrawn under this plan must be repaid on a non-deductible basis over 15 years (1/15 each year), starting in tax year 1995, for those who participated before March 2, 1994. Revenue Canada will send you a notice with the repayment amount required. If you participate in 1998, your first repayment must begin in the year 2000. It will end in the year 2014. The taxpayer may choose to repay the amounts more quickly than scheduled, if desired. However, if you miss making at least these minimum repayments, an income inclusion for any shortfall will result. You have until 60 days after the calendar year end to make the repayment. You can designate this on Schedule 7.

You cannot designate a Spousal RRSP contribution as a repayment of the HBP, or any amounts of direct rollovers, such as retiring allowances. It is not necessary, though, to have an RRSP deduction limit in order to designate a repayment.

For those who wish to participate in the plan in 1998, the procedure begins with an RRSP withdrawal using Form T1036. This form is given to your RRSP issuer, who will then know not to withhold any taxes from your withdrawal. You can only participate in 1998 if you have never participated before, as this is a "once in a lifetime" opportunity. To qualify you must be a resident of Canada and you must have entered into an agreement to buy a home or to build one. Finally, you must buy or build your home before October 1, 1999.

If the home buyer dies, the balance owed at the time of death will be included in the deceased's income. However, the surviving spouse can elect to assume the repayment schedule to avoid this liability. However, the election can only be made if

- only the deceased was participating in the HBP
- only the surviving spouse was participating (but the deceased had applied)
- the spouses each had identical repayment periods.

Should the home buyer become a non-resident, no tax inclusion will occur if the balance outstanding is repaid before filing a tax return for the year of departure and within 60 days of becoming a non-resident. After 1997 no repayments are allowed after the end of the calendar year in which you reach 69 years of age. Also check into any additional, tax credit-producing "home buyers plan" that may be available in your home province.

152 WRITE OFF YOUR HOME OWNERSHIP COSTS

Once you have saved the downpayment for your home or second residence, put that property to work for you. By arranging your affairs, you could have new income sources subsidize at least a part of your mortgage payments, taxes and other operating expenses.

You might run a small business out of your home. In that case, you can deduct a portion of your mortgage interest, property taxes, utilities, repairs and maintenance, insurance and other supply costs, based on the square footage of the home workspace, over the total living area in the home. Provided you do not claim Capital Cost Allowance on your home as a home workspace deduction, your principal residence exemption will stay fully intact. In the meantime, you will be using these legitimate tax deductions to reduce the tax you pay on the small business venture.

153 RENT OUT A PORTION OF YOUR HOME

If practical, you can have others supplement your home ownership costs. You might, for example, also decide to rent out a part of your principal residence. In general, when you start using your residence as a rental property, you are deemed to have disposed of that portion of the property at a fair market value. Such a disposition can have tax consequences when you subsequently sell the home, or if you have selected another residence to be the "principal residence" in the pre-rental period.

However, there is no deemed "change of use" if the portion of the home that is rented is minor, no major structural changes are made to accommodate tenants and no deduction is taken for Capital Cost Allowance on the rented part. In this case, your tax exempt principal residence status is preserved completely.

Any time your home or part of it is converted into a self-contained domestic apartment used to rent to tenants, that part of the home will no longer qualify for the tax exempt status, even though no CCA claim is made.

You may also move out of the principal residence and earn rental income from it for up to four years as long as you do not designate any other property to be your principal residence in this period and again no Capital Cost Allowance deduction is made on the property. This election may be extended beyond the four-year period in cases where your employer requires you to relocate to a new temporary residence at least 40 kilometres away, as long as you return to your original home before the end of the year in which your employment ends (see later comments).

154 MAXIMIZE YOUR RENTAL PROPERTY EARNINGS TO CREATE NEW MONEY

For those taxpayers who have invested in a rental property that is not also a principal residence, take note of the following tax savings rules, which can help you minimize the taxes payable:

1. Rental income and expenses are usually reported on a calendar-year basis, using the cash method.
2. Net income is first calculated by reducing gross rental income by operating expenses.
3. Operating expenses that exceed gross earnings create a rental loss, which can be used to offset other income of the year.

4. Capital Cost Allowance may be claimed to reduce net income to nil; however, CCA may not be used to create or increase a rental loss.

5. CCA is claimed at the taxpayer's option. Therefore, depreciating a building far below its market value may result in a recapture of previously taken CCA deductions upon disposition of all the assets in the class.

6. Claiming CCA on a principal residence disqualifies the property (or the portion of the property upon which CCA is claimed) from its normal tax-exempt status.

Net rental income is eligible "earned income" used in calculating RRSP contribution room.

155 BE SURE TO AUDIT-PROOF YOUR RENTAL INCOME

Revenue Canada has become particularly concerned with those who write off rental losses against other income, from enterprises that include rentals to relatives or other non-arm's length persons. To avoid unpleasant reassessments in the future, be sure that you are using Fair Market Value pricing in all rental charges. Know what the income level for similar rental properties is in the same neighbourhood. Document this with newspaper clippings of ads for vacant rental spaces, or listings by real estate or leasing agents. Keep all receipts and documents.

156 VACANT LAND CAN BE INCOME-PRODUCING

Taxpayers who earn rental income from vacant land can claim property taxes and interest only to the extent of rental income reported — again, no rental loss can be created or increased with these expenses. They may, however, be added to the land's adjusted cost base for use in calculating any subsequent capital gain or loss on disposition.

However, if the vacant land is held without any rental income being collected, interest and property taxes can neither be deducted nor added to the adjusted cost base.

157 KNOW HOW TO TRANSFER ASSETS AMONGST FAMILY MEMBERS

Taxpayers often wish to pass their residences on to other family members. You can do so during your lifetime (*inter vivos*) or it may be forced upon the family by virtue of your death, when a deemed disposition at Fair Market Value (FMV) is considered to have taken place.

At death, tax-free transfer can be made between spouses. That is, on the final return assets can be transferred to the spouse at their Adjusted Cost Base (ACB) if you wish. In the case of taxable properties, your executor may elect to transfer the asset to your spouse at its FMV, if this is to the family's advantage.

In general, all transfers to children must be at the asset's Fair Market Value. On the final return the difference between the ACB and the FMV is reported by the owner as a capital gain, except in the case of a principal residence, when the resulting gain is considered to be tax exempt.

When you transfer taxable assets to your spouse or children during your lifetime you must be very careful to avoid the Attribution Rules on the subsequent use or sale of the asset by your dependents.

Sales of taxable property transferred to your spouse will result in attribution of the capital gains back to you, unless you have previously elected to transfer the property at FMV and paid the tax at that time. Alternatively, you could set up a bona fide loan which is repayable by your spouse, within 30 days of the year end, and interest is set, charged and paid at least at Revenue Canada's prescribed rates.

Capital Gains on sales of property transferred to your children are handled differently.

158 THERE ARE TAX ADVANTAGES OF ASSET TRANSFERS TO CHILDREN

It makes sense to give to your minor child or grandchild a mutual fund or other capital asset instead of a Canada Savings Bond or GIC, particularly if the asset's value is at a current low.

This is because the Attribution Rules do not apply to capital gains income on disposition of assets transferred to a child. While you'll have to report the original transfer of the asset at Fair Market Value for your tax purposes, the child then reports the resulting capital gains on the future sale of that asset. Timing of this transaction can therefore be matched to each person's best tax advantage.

Unfortunately, though, certain income sources, including interest or dividends earned from the gift of a capital asset to a minor child will be taxed in the hands of the adult who gave the gift, until that child turns 18. Therefore in giving assets that have capital, rather than income growth potential over the years to age 18, income splitting can be achieved and the child can benefit from the tax-deferred accrued investment gains, until actual disposition.

159 ENHANCE INSURANCE PROCEEDS TO COVER TAX ON ASSETS

In the year a taxpayer dies, s/he is considered to have disposed of all capital property immediately prior to death, usually at fair market value. Such a valuation will generally invoke a capital gain or loss. In the case of depreciable property (property upon which a Capital Cost Allowance deduction could be taken), it can also create a terminal loss or recapture, depending upon the amount of the Undepreciated Capital Cost (UCC).

The executor often has a series of choices to make in this valuation exercise in order to minimize tax on the final return of the deceased, and to plan the future tax position of the beneficiary of the assets.

Remember, assets can usually be "rolled over" to a spouse at their Adjusted Cost Base — what the deceased acquired it for plus any capital additions while s/he owned it — or UCC, if depreciable. A special election may be made to choose FMV if this is to the family's advantage.

With the removal of the $100,000 Capital Gains Deduction, capital gains on second family residences or other assets could result in expensive tax liabilities. Consider enhancing life insurance coverage for the surviving spouse to protect your assets from being sold by your children in order to pay the resulting capital gains taxes. Professional help should be sought to forecast the approximate amount of tax and insurance coverage necessary in these cases.

Also be sure that all unused capital losses incurred during your lifetime are carried forward, to offset capital gains generated by the "deemed disposition at death" rules.

160 USE THE CAPITAL GAINS ELECTION INFORMATION

In the 1994 tax filing year, taxpayers and accountants alike struggled with the complexity of the Capital Gains Election. With all the calculations filed and in place, it is now important to know how to interpret them for future use.

Here's how to use the new Adjusted Cost Base information, if you must report the disposition of an asset upon which you made an election:

1. If the property is an interest in a flow-through entity, such as a mutual fund, the elected capital gains will form part of an "exempt gains pool," which will shelter capital gains that flowed out after February 22, 1994. These offsetting amounts will be subtracted from capital gains on a special line on Schedule 3: Capital Gains and Losses.

2. In most other cases, the Adjusted Cost Base of the asset will be the amount of the elected "proceeds" designated in the election, less any non-eligible gain in non-qualifying real property. This refers to the portion of the capital gain in non-commercial real estate that accrued in the period March 1992 to February 1994.

3. For non-qualifying real property that is designated a principal residence after 1994, the original adjusted cost base will be used in calculating the gain on actual disposition. The principal residence exemption will then be calculated on Form T2091, and any previously reported gain under the Capital Gains Election will be subtracted from the actual gain on disposition. Again, remember to take into account any ineligible portion of the gain for non-qualifying real property.

4. For principal residences that continue to be considered "taxable second residences" after the election, any future capital gain will be calculated as actual proceeds of disposition less the elected proceeds less any ineligible portion of the capital gain reported in 1994.

It may be best to seek professional guidance in completing these rather complicated transactions.

CHAPTER 9

START YOUR PRE-RETIREMENT PLANNING

Do you know...

* *You can plan to minimize taxes on your retiring allowances...*
* *You can ask for perks of employment to continue past retirement...*
* *You can negotiate a tax-free death benefit...*
* *You can custom-design your pension benefits to minimize taxes...*
* *You can claim special tax provisions if in receipt of foreign pensions...*
* *You can influence the size of your public pension benefits by planning now...*

As you drive along life's winding road, with your roadmap for success ever at your side, your destination — retirement — comes closer and closer.

For most young Canadians — busy with their education, careers and families — there is little time to focus on that seemingly distant place beyond the horizon. However, sooner or later we do arrive at a point in our lives when the future is now.

The length and difficulty of our journey through life can, to a large degree, determine the quality of life we will have in our retirement years. If we are lucky enough to keep our health, our personal productivity can help us achieve a higher level of security or independence. However, if disability, death, divorce or other major misfortunes have come our way, our financial resources must produce the earnings to determine our life-style. Therefore, the key to a worry-free future is to do some planning — for the expected and the unexpected — now.

161 INSURE YOUR MOST IMPORTANT ASSETS, INCLUDING YOURSELF

Funny, how people think. Most will have no problem agreeing that their vehicles must have annual check-ups, go through maintenance programs and be insured in case of loss or damage. How many of us feel the same way about our well-being?

The truth is, the most important income-producing asset most people have is themselves! One of the most important steps in creating wealth and maintaining it, to the extent to which you have control over such things, is to preserve your health throughout your lifetime. *Plan* to be productive and healthy. Regardless of age, your family's living standards will suffer if you don't take care of yourself.

While you have your health, you must think about what will happen to your living standards when you no longer can produce. Insure yourself for the possibility of disability or death. It is important to have financial resources at hand for the periods in your life when your actively generated income earning capacity has stopped or ended.

From a tax point of view, this is also wise. For example, the life insurance policy proceeds you leave for your family in the case of your untimely death, will be completely tax free to your beneficiaries. While it may be difficult to come up with the after-tax dollars to fund such a policy, you might consider taking the tax savings from your RRSP investments and turning them over — at least in part — to the investment in a life insurance product. Speak to your financial advisors about your options. Remember, the time to buy life insurance is when you are healthy. It's tough — or incredibly expensive — to get insurance if you are afflicted with a serious illness or old age.

Insurance for disability is just as important. While there is some protection under the Canada Pension Plan, and in some cases, the Employment Insurance Plan, receiving the benefits can take a long period of time, while the government determines your eligibility. By making plans to contribute premiums to a private disability insurance plan, benefits, when needed, can be received on a tax-free basis. Premiums paid, however, are not tax deductible in this case.

If you have an opportunity to contribute to a wage-loss replacement plan through your employment, be sure to enquire about the details of the plan, should you need to draw from it. Will benefits be taxable? Will benefits continue until you are able to do exactly the same job, or will they discontinue if the insurance company deems you are fit to work again — at any job? Some planning for all of these possibilities will certainly pay off, as you don't want to be negotiating when you are at your weakest — or sickest.

162 NEGOTIATE YOUR SEVERANCE PACKAGE UP FRONT

Have you ever tried to negotiate overdraft protection when you're unemployed, or a line of credit after posting a business loss? It can be difficult, if not impossible.

It can be equally difficult to negotiate a retiring allowance once you've been laid off or terminated. It's when times are good that you should look to the future and negotiate the terms of your "golden handshake."

Revenue Canada has allowed a special tax deferral (explained below) for those who receive a "retiring allowance," which can include severance pay, unused sick leave, termination damages and legal fees deductibility. But the deferral opportunity is not available for service after 1995. Employees will want to make sure Revenue Canada has not taken back a big chunk of the retiring package at tax time by planning retirement packages well in advance.

163 DEFER AS MUCH TAX AS POSSIBLE ON YOUR RETIRING ALLOWANCE WITH AN RRSP TRANSFER

A taxpayer is allowed to roll over, into his or her own RRSP, a portion of a retiring allowance received up to a maximum of $2,000 per year of service after 1988, and before 1996. An additional $1,500, for a total of $3,500, may be transferred for each year of service prior to 1989, in which an employer's contributions to a company pension plan had not vested in the taxpayer. This could have happened during a period of temporary employment with your company.

Outside of these parameters, any remaining balance of the retiring allowance you've received will be "ineligible" for contribution to the RRSP and are, as such, fully taxable. Take the time to calculate the tax benefits achieved through the skillful use of the "rollover" of the retiring allowance, as well as unused RRSP contribution room, in order to minimize tax on this important final payment. (See Tip 165.)

164 WATCH OUT FOR THE MINIMUM TAX

When a retiring allowance is rolled over into an RRSP, it could trigger a minimum tax balance. The minimum tax is a special calculation, performed "off the tax return" on Form T691, available from Revenue Canada. The minimum tax was introduced in the late 1980s to ensure that those who take advantage of otherwise legal "tax preferences," such as the RRSP rollover on termination, would pay at least a minimum amount of tax.

The good news is that even if you are subject to pay minimum tax, you'll be able to carry it forward the next seven years as a credit against regular taxes payable. This is a provision that most people in this situation are unaware of, and as a result, it costs them dearly. You can find reference to the minimum tax carry-over provision on Schedule 1, The Detailed Tax Calculation, found with the T1 General Guide package. If you have missed claiming the carryover in the past, you can request an adjustment to those prior-filed returns. It's a good idea to seek professional help before you accept a severance package, to ensure you are aware of potential minimum tax risk and your rights to recover any such taxes paid.

165 OFFSET ANY UNSHELTERED RETIRING ALLOWANCE WITH YOUR RRSP ROOM

In the year you retire, you will likely have an opportunity to make a "regular" RRSP contribution, based on your accumulated "Unused RRSP Contribution Room." If you've received a retiring allowance that exceeds the tax-deferral limitations discussed above, this untapped "room" can save you money. This is particularly important in light of the end of the RRSP rollover eligibility of service after 1995.

Let's say, for example, that you qualify to receive a $25,000 retiring allowance, of which $16,000 is transferable into your RRSP. The remaining $9,000 must be added into your income in the year received. You may be able to negotiate the receipt of the non-eligible allowance in January of the new year, so that it forms part of your income in the next tax year when your overall earnings are lower.

By transferring the other $16,000 received during the current tax year directly from your employer to the RRSP, you will avoid income tax source deductions. On the tax return the $16,000 is first reported as income, and then the $16,000 transfer is reported as an RRSP deduction, which is allowed over and above the normal RRSP contribution room.

Now assume you also have RRSP contribution room of $8,000. By investing this amount into an RRSP in the year in which you can use the deduction to offset the ineligible allowance, you receive a further $8,000 tax deduction, with the result that all but $1,000 of the retiring allowance is sheltered from tax. These moves will ensure that most of your retiring allowance stays in your pocket. Don't forget: prepare a minimum tax calculation as well.

166 CONSIDER NEGOTIATING FOR TAX-FREE BENEFITS

You are probably already convinced that it doesn't pay to skimp on the tax advice you need when negotiating your retirement package. Here is more good news: your employer can provide you with the money to seek retirement counselling, including financial counselling, on a tax-free basis. This is a perk that should be negotiated when you receive your employment contract at the start of your relationship, if possible.

You might also ask for — and receive — memberships to recreational facilities on a tax-free basis, or the payment of premiums for private health services, or even a low-interest loan, to continue even after your employment terminates.

167 KEEP INCOME AND BENEFITS FLOWING AFTER TERMINATION

It is not uncommon for employees to negotiate a consulting contract with their former employer after their employment ends. This puts you into a self-employment status, with a completely new tax filing profile. Net self-employment income also qualifies for the purposes of building RRSP Room, so that you can continue to enhance your retirement savings.

In such a situation it may be possible to negotiate for the continued use of certain taxable benefits. (Usually a T4A Slip would be issued in such cases.)

But be very careful. Revenue Canada could disallow the tax-free RRSP rollover of your severance package if they determine that you didn't really "retire." Subsequent consulting contracts must not be a replacement of the employment you previously had.

168 NEGOTIATE A TAX-SHELTERED DEATH BENEFIT

When negotiating an employment contract, prepare for your family's future by enquiring about the possibility of receiving a death benefit. Such a lump-sum payment might be made to your spouse or dependants as a recognition of your service, should you pass away while on the job.

There is a lucrative tax exemption on death benefits paid by the employer: the first $10,000 received by your dependants is not subject to tax.

If your death benefit exceeds $10,000, plan to have the excess paid out over a period of years, which will minimize the tax your dependants will pay on the unexempted or taxable amounts.

. While all income sources are appreciated during the stressful events surrounding the death of a loved one, a lump-sum death benefit is particularly advantageous if it can be received to offset the otherwise non-deductible costs of a funeral.

169 MAXIMIZE CPP BENEFITS FOR YOURSELF AND YOUR SURVIVORS

It is important to factor any CPP Benefits into your pre-retirement planning activities. By the time you reach age 60, you can choose to tap into your Canada Pension Plan to receive a retirement benefit. Or, if you can, wait to age 65, or even 70, when retirement benefits must start. The amounts receivable depend upon the contributions you make to the CPP during your lifetime, and how early you start receiving benefits. When the benefits start, they become fully taxable.

When a contributor to the Canada Pension Plan passes away, the spouse will qualify for a Lump-Sum Death Benefit and a Survivor's Benefit. Both of these amounts are taxable to the *survivor* in the year to which the payment relates, or the lump sum may be claimed on a return filed by the estate.

Dependent children will also qualify to receive Orphan or Child Benefits. These amounts are taxable to the children. They should be invested in an account of the child, so that resulting investment earnings are taxed in the hands of the child rather than the surviving adult. This is a legitimate way to avoid the Attribution Rules. (Only children 18 and over will receive a T4A(P) Slip.)

And, should you become permanently disabled, a CPP Disability Benefit may be payable to you and your minor dependent children. If you are not already doing so, you should try to maximize your contributions while you are employed or self-employed, to enhance CPP payable to you when you need it.

170 CUSTOM DESIGN YOUR RRSP PENSION INCOME

After a lifetime of saving your pre-tax dollars, the time will one day come to make your RRSP withdrawals, as discussed below. It is important to note that both principal and interest from the RRSP will be subject to 100% income inclusion when you do withdraw. It is therefore always preferable to plan withdrawals over a period of years.

Peter, aged 50, is single and has no dependants. He has accumulated $200,000 in his RRSP. He has a comfortable lifestyle due to a pension from his former company, investments and the fact that he has very few expenses. He knows that, upon his death, his RRSP will be deemed disposed of and added to his income, in which case about one-half of the accumulations will be paid to the government by way of taxes — money that could be better sheltered and invested during his lifetime.

Peter may wish to plan for an orderly withdrawal of his RRSP accumulations now to minimize taxes payable over the balance of his lifetime and upon death. He may also wish to enhance his plans for charitable giving. (See Tip 173.) He should therefore speak to his financial planner about a custom-designed pension plan.

171 RRSP WITHDRAWAL MUST BEGIN AFTER AGE 69

Most pensioners seek tax deferrals, as pension income and investment income sources are not considered to be "earned income" for RRSP purposes, and are included in taxable income in the year received.

Therefore, unless you earn income from part-time employment, or a small business you might start out of your home, pay taxable child or spousal support or earn net rental income you might receive from a revenue property, your RRSP contribution room will cease for future years.

You will then have to deal with making RRSP withdrawals in some cases. The effect of these rules is that every year after turning 69 you will pay tax on at least a minimum amount of withdrawals from a Registered Retirement Income Fund (RRIF) or annuity. It can pay to plan your income levels in advance of this deadline.

A taxpayer, for example, may contribute to an RRSP in each year in which there is unused RRSP contribution room from prior years, up until the end of the year in which he or she turns 69.

If over age 69, you can still contribute to an RRSP if you have the required contribution room, but only to a spousal RRSP, provided that your spouse is under that age limit. In such cases, you can write off the spousal contribution on your own return. Using these options, you might plan to offset retiring allowances, CPP Benefits and RRIF payments to optimize your RRSP contributions.

172 WORK AROUND THE THREE-YEAR HOLDING RULES

When you make an RRSP contribution to a Spousal Plan, the spouse will be able to report the withdrawals in the future, provided that the amounts remain in the plan for at least three years from the last spousal contribution.

These "three-year" rules will not apply in the year the contributor dies; where the withdrawal is made due to marriage breakdown at a time the taxpayer and spouse are living apart; where the taxpayers were non-residents of Canada; or where the amount was directly transferred to another RRSP, RRIF or annuity that cannot be commuted (paid out) for at least three years.

Special rules also apply where the spouse transfers the amounts in the Spousal RRSP into a RRIF. In such cases any amounts withdrawn over and above the minimum required withdrawal will be taxed in the contributor spouse's hands until the holding requirement is met. You may wish to plan your withdrawals around these provisions to minimize the family's tax burden.

✸ 173 MAXIMIZE YOUR CHARITABLE DONATIONS WITH RRSP INCOME

The earlier you plan your RRSP withdrawals, the more opportunity you will have for tax savings.

If you know you won't need the money, and you will have no surviving family member to leave it to, consider making withdrawals to maximize amounts you can give to charity. Deductible charitable donations are limited to 75% of your net income, with any restricted portion over and above this carried forward for five years. In addition, 25% of any taxable capital gains resulting from the gifts of capital property plus

25% of any recapture of depreciation included as income as a result of making such gifts will be added to the net income limitation.

Also, donations of certain publicly traded shares will now qualify for a reduced income inclusion rate of 37.5% upon their deemed disposition to the charity, if these donations were made after February 18, 1997 and before the year 2002. You may wish to speak to your financial advisor about this.

In the year you die and the year immediately preceding, charitable donations claims may be as high as 100% of your net income. Your executors may choose to deduct excess donations in the year of death or the immediately preceding year, or both.

You might, therefore, plan your RRSP withdrawals to achieve net income levels that allow you to maximize your charitable donations over a period of years, particularly if you have no heirs.

174 KNOW THE IMMEDIATE COST OF RRSP WITHDRAWAL

The object behind an RRSP is to contribute to it when your tax bracket is high and withdraw from it when you are in a lower one.

Many taxpayers are surprised that it costs them money immediately to access their RRSP accumulations. When you withdraw money from your RRSP tax will be withheld: 10% if the amount is $5,000 or less; 20% between $5,001 and $15,000; and 30% if you withdraw more than $15,000. Plan for this if you are using the fund for a specific purpose.

An "unmatured" RRSP (that is, one that is not yet paying you a retirement income), must be withdrawn or transferred into either an annuity or a Registered Retirement Income Fund (RRIF) before the end of the year in which you turn age 69. If you transfer amounts directly from an RRSP to an annuity or RRIF. You can arrange for periodic income from the plan, which is taxed in the year received.

You can "mature" an RRSP at any time before you yourself reach the magic maturity age. Or you can simply withdraw lump sums, at your option, as renewal terms come up. You should plan renewal terms to minimize your tax liability, by knowing and understanding your marginal tax bracket.

175 PLAN TO NAME YOUR SPOUSE AS THE BENEFICIARY OF YOUR RRSP

The fair market value of your RRSP must be included in your income in the year of death; however, a tax-free transfer of the RRSP accumulations is allowed if your spouse or common-law spouse is named as the beneficiary. That is, your spouse can choose to "roll over" the RRSP into his or her own RRSP.

If your spouse is not the beneficiary of the RRSP specifically, but is the beneficiary of the estate, the legal representative can elect with the spouse to treat the amounts as a "refund of premiums" payable to your spouse. These amounts will be deemed received by your spouse in the same calendar year they were paid to the estate, with the result that an RRSP again may be transferred to the spouse's RRSP. A special form must be filed in this case (T2019).

If there is no surviving spouse, but financially dependent children or grandchildren, amounts from your RRSP may be treated as a "refund of premiums" that are transferable to the dependant's RRSP, or annuity, depending on whether or not the child is infirm. Those children who are infirm can only buy a term annuity. Speak to your tax advisor if this is a concern for you.

176 MANAGE YOUR PERSONAL RESIDENCES IN RETIREMENT

It is not uncommon to own several real properties in your middle age: a summer cottage, a home in the Sunbelt, and perhaps a condo in the city for the "in between" months, or a revenue property that is inhabited only by tenants.

Provided that the rental income received is at fair market value, reported in Canadian funds, and a profit motive exists, you may be able to deduct from other income of the year any rental loss incurred. Where it is clear the intent of the purchase or change in use of the property was income-producing rather than personal use, gains on disposition would be taxable.

However, be very careful not to compromise the tax-exempt status of one principal residence per family unit. At tax time, ask your tax advisor to help you define, on an annual basis, your tax-exempt principal residence, as described in Tip 177.

177 PRESERVE PRINCIPAL RESIDENCE STATUS ON VACATION PROPERTIES

If you only receive a small or incidental amount of income from your vacation property, it is not considered to be owned for the purposes of earning income and, therefore, could be considered to be your tax-exempt principal residence as long as you "ordinarily inhabited" the property at some time during the year.

Where there are two family residences, the principal residence designation can be made on an annual basis. The taxpayer can choose which property to claim for the taxable status on disposition, depending on which appreciated more during the time it was "ordinarily inhabited" by the taxpayer.

178 KEEP YOUR PROPERTY VALUES UPDATED

To help you decide whether to sell or transfer your residences, or if you are considering a change of use in your properties, be sure you have an updated valuation of your assets at hand. Use this checklist to do so.

❏ Prepare a list describing each property owned.

❏ Accumulate the following data to use in calculating any tax exempt portion for time the property was used as a personal residence:

  1. Number of years owned after 1971,

  2. Number of years owned after 1981,

  3. Amount of Capital Gains Election and ineligible portion of elected gain. (From your 1994 tax return.)

❏ Use of Property for each year owned:

  1. Personal enjoyment: from _____ to _____

  2. Rental income: from _____ to _____

  3. Business income: from _____ to _____

❏ Valuation of Property (attach supporting documentation):

  1. On acquisition: _____

  2. On change of use: _____

  3. Cost of major additions: _____

  4. As at December 31, 1971:   _____

  5. As at December 31, 1981:   _____

  6. As at February 22, 1994:   _____

  7. On disposition: _____

❏ Ownership Details: List the properties owned by each spouse, breaking out those that have been transferred without consideration and those that are owned by the spouse in his or her own right.

179 CAPITAL COST ALLOWANCE CAN REDUCE INCOME TO NIL

If your property is an income-producing property, Capital Cost Allowance may be claimed on the building, based on its acquisition costs and the costs of any additions or improvements. Remember that if Capital

Cost Allowance is claimed on a property you inhabit, you automatically forfeit any principal residence status for the "business portion" of the residence. The CCA deduction cannot create or increase a rental loss. CCA rates and classes for buildings are the following:

Buildings acquired after 1987:	Class 1:	4%
Buildings acquired before 1988:	Class 3:	5%
Furniture and Fixtures,	Class 8:	20%

In the year of acquisition, be sure to separate the value of the building from the value of the land, as land cannot be depreciated. One way to do this is to request the property tax assessment notice, which will break out these costs according to the city assessment. Also, be sure to add on the cost of legal fees paid on acquisition to the total cost before the proration for CCA purposes.

180 SCHEDULE BUILDINGS COSTING $50,000 OR MORE SEPARATELY

If you own several rental properties, there are special tax filing rules to observe. Every building costing $50,000 or more must be placed in a separate Class for depreciation purposes, except if two or more condo units are owned in the same building, in which case the condos are considered part of the same building.

As well, the half-year rule applies to all buildings acquired: in the year of acquisition, only one-half the usual CCA rate can be claimed. Be prepared to provide your tax advisor with the appropriate information.

181 KNOW WHETHER TO EXPENSE OR CAPITALIZE RENTAL COSTS

The most expensive error a taxpayer can make in reporting rental income and expenses is to write off in full expenditures that are obviously capital (depreciable) in nature. Ask the following questions to make the correct determination:

1. Does the expense extend the useful life of the property? If yes, it is generally considered a capital expenditure.
2. Does the expense recur after a short period of time? If so, it is probably a fully deductible operating expense.
3. Does the expense restore the property to its original condition? If so, it is probably a current expense, especially if the amounts are under $200.

4. Does the expenditure improve upon the original condition of the property? If yes, capitalize the item.

182 CLAIM YOUR AUTOMOBILE EXPENSES IF YOU MAINTAIN PROPERTIES

Revenue Canada has specific rules for the claiming of auto expenses against rental income. Auto expenses are generally only deductible if *two or more properties* are owned. Taxpayers with only one rental property may deduct auto costs for maintenance and repair work personally performed on the property by the owner, but only if the property is situated near the owner's residence.

Therefore, if you have an owner who rents his property because he lives or works 300 kilometres away, car trips for maintenance and repairs will not be allowed.

183 OFFICE IN HOME CLAIM MAY BE MADE AGAINST RENTAL INCOME

If the property owner uses a home office space for bookkeeping, placing ads, interviewing prospective tenants, meeting tenants for lease negotiations, etc., a claim may be made based on business use of operating expenses, the extent of the operations, the time involved using the office, etc. Revenue Canada would likely consider a single property operation insufficient to warrant a home office claim. However, office stationery expenses would be deductible in that case.

184 KNOW ABOUT OTHER TAX-DEDUCTIBLE EXPENSES FOR RENTAL PROPERTY OWNERS

Save receipts for the following tax-deductible expenditures and claim them on your tax return, if you own a rental property:

- accounting fees
- advertising
- commissions paid to leasing agents
- finder's fees paid in arranging a loan or mortgage. (The expense is deductible in equal portions over five years, unless it is paid sooner. In that case, the balance of the expense is deductible in the year the mortgage is repaid.)
- insurance premiums for current year insurance coverage
- interest on money borrowed to purchase or improve your property, or interest paid to tenants on their rental deposits

- landscaping costs
- lease cancellation payments (amortize these over the remaining life of the lease to a maximum of 40 years)
- maintenance, repairs and utilities
- office in the home (more than one property) and stationery costs
- property taxes
- salary paid to those who supervise the properties.

185 FOREIGN EXCHANGE CAN INCREASE OR DECREASE YOUR INCOME

Canadian residents must report "world income" in Canadian funds on their tax returns.

If money you receive from a foreign source can be classified as "income" in nature (i.e., rental income), then any gains resulting from foreign exchange is considered to be taxable income to you.

However, if the gain in foreign exchange results from a "capital" transaction (i.e., when you sell the property itself and incur a capital gain), foreign exchange gains or losses are treated as capital gains or losses.

A $200 exemption is allowed for foreign currency gains on certain capital transactions.

186 KNOW THE TAX RULES BEHIND DISPOSITION OF PRINCIPAL RESIDENCES

The exempt principal residence status of your home can change if you start using it for income-producing purposes (i.e., for rental or business purposes).

Whenever there is a change in use, there is a deemed disposition at fair market value and an immediate reacquisition at the same fair market value. Any gain on such a disposition is reduced by each year the property was designated to be a principal residence. If the home was your principal residence every year before you changed its use, no tax is due on any resulting capital gain until the property is actually sold.

You might also convert an income-producing property to a principal residence. Again, a deemed disposition is considered to have occurred at fair market value, and a special election can be made to defer the gain, as described below.

187 DEFER CAPITAL GAINS WITH SPECIAL ELECTIONS

You can elect to defer a capital gain on a principal residence if you move out of it and rent it. Under Section 45(2) of the Income Tax Act, you can elect to have the property remain your principal residence throughout the time it is rented, as long as you report your rental income and allowable expenses, and do not claim any capital cost allowance on the home.

The election will stay in effect until you dispose of the property or cancel the election. The property can be designated to be your principal residence for up to four years during the election period. Extensions of the four-year limitation are available in some instances.

If you change your rental property to a principal residence, an election under Section 45(3) of the Act will allow you to defer any capital gain on the deemed disposition until the home is actually sold. This election will not apply to any recaptured depreciation stemming from the change in use.

188 BE AWARE OF THE NEW SENIORS BENEFIT

The March 6, 1996 federal budget introduced the proposed new Seniors Benefit, a plan to replace the Old Age Security, which is currently paid on a universal basis, with an income-tested government pension that will be received tax free by qualifying taxpayers. The new system is proposed to *begin for most seniors in 2001;* however, anyone who turned 60 by December 31, 1995 may elect to remain in the current OAS system for the rest of their lives, if that is beneficial (see comments below).

The Seniors Benefit will incorporate the current OAS/Guaranteed Income Supplement (GIS) provisions, the Age Credit and the Pension Income Amount. These latter two provisions will therefore disappear off the return when the new system is in place.

It is important for upper middle-income Canadians to prepare for the effects of the proposed new system. For example, under the current system, each individual spouse's net income can be as high $53,215 (or combined $106,430) before a clawback of OAS takes place in the tax return. Elimination of the OAS occurs when the couple's income reaches $170,000 (that's about $85,000 for singles).

Under the new Seniors Benefit, payments will stop completely once a couple's net income reaches $78,000 ($52,000 in the case of singles). The clawback rate is also accelerated under the new system.

Those who turned 60 in 1995 may choose between the revised OAS system (with the elimination of the Age and Pension Income Amounts) or the new Seniors Benefit. While every income scenario might produce slightly different results, the following general conclusions can be drawn based on information available at the time of writing, to help with this decision:

1. For those families whose net family income is under $25,921, the new Seniors Benefit will give slightly more benefits than the current OAS system. This is primarily because the Seniors Benefit will be received on a tax free basis, and as a result, can increase the Spousal Amount for some couples.

2. Middle-income families will see erosion under the proposed new systems, whether they choose to stay with the revised OAS or switch to the Seniors Benefit. However, in the case of married couples, it could be more advantageous to choose the new Seniors Benefit over the revised OAS system, because of the advantages under the Spousal Amount.

3. At upper- and high-income brackets, taxpayers will be better off staying with the revised OAS system. The rate at which the Seniors Benefit is clawed back and the net family income levels at which the clawback begin are accelerated under the new SB.

It would, therefore, be important to try to plan as far in advance as possible to make up any shortfall in overall pension income due to the changes proposed to our public pension system, with investment planning. Find out what the erosion will be, how your tax affairs will be affected, and what you can do now to maximize your Seniors Benefits in the future. This might include a switch to equities in your investment portfolio or a reconsideration of how pension withdrawals from an RRSP or RRIF may be timed.

★189 REPORTING RULES FOR U.S. SOCIAL SECURITY CHANGE AGAIN

New in '97

Under the new Canada – U.S. protocol, pensions are taxed at their source. In the 1996 and 1997 tax filing year, Revenue Canada required that the full amount of U.S. Social Security pension received must be included as income on the Canadian tax return, in Canadian funds, even though recipients were subject to a withholding tax in the United States. Then a deduction for the full amount of the income reported was made on line 256, rendering the pension almost fully tax exempt, except for the effect it had on refundable tax credits and net income taxes in certain provinces, due to the resulting increased net income levels.

Complaints by lower-income earners caused Canada and the U.S. to consider changes to the tax treatment of U.S. Social Security income in Canada. These latest changes, however, will be less advantageous to higher-income earners.

Under the proposed new rules, Canadian recipients will receive 100% of their U.S. Social Security from the United States (that is, when this change is ratified, the U.S. will stop withholding taxes). While the full amount of these benefits will be included in income on the Canadian return (in Canadian funds, of course). There will be an offsetting deduction on Line 256 of only 15%.

As a result, 1996 and 1997 tax returns will be automatically reassessed by Revenue Canada, and any refunds owing to Canadians will be refunded without the need for special applications, according to information available at the time of writing. Best to check with your local Tax Services office about finalized procedures before filing your 1997 tax return.

Other foreign pension income sources have different tax treatment. For example, British pensions are fully taxable. However, in the case of certain German pensions, the full amount received is reported on line 115 of the return; then an offsetting deduction is taken at line 256. Again, convert the income to Canadian funds. The result is that these foreign pensions will increase net income but not taxable income.

Canadians who emigrate, on the other hand, must now file a special tax form (T1 Old Age Security Return) and report their world income in order to continue to receive their CPP and OAS abroad.

CHAPTER 10

KEEP MORE OF YOUR PENSION INCOME

Do you know...

* *You can manage your quarterly tax instalments to increase cash flow...*
* *You can split the reporting of CPP benefits received between spouses...*
* *You can decrease your OAS Clawback in hardship cases...*
* *The new Refundable Medical Expense Supplement can help you pay for expensive medications...*

Retirement. For many this is a period of adjustment and change, both personally and financially. It can be a new beginning of promise and self-actualization. It can also bring with it the physical and financial challenges of aging. Not surprisingly, there are also significant income tax consequences.

Harold recently retired from a career as a real estate agent. He looked up and smiled when his first Old Age Security cheque appeared in the mailbox. "First steady income I've ever had!" he smirked. Harold's generation is perhaps the last that can make this kind of a statement. With the forthcoming erosion of public pensions under the proposed Seniors Benefit, younger Canadians must be prepared to finance their own retirements. This task comes at a time of unprecedentedly high tax rates in Canada, meaning that there are fewer after-tax dollars to save. As well, increased publicly funded fees for use of the public medicare system constitute potential financial burdens for those whose retirement is mired in illness.

Therefore, the tax-filing profile of senior Canadians is unique, and filled with important planning opportunities for tax savings...

190 LEARN TO ANTICIPATE QUARTERLY INSTALMENT REMITTANCE REQUIREMENTS

One of the major changes in cash flow planning for seniors is the responsibility they have to remit their own tax instalment payments. The government requires prepayments of tax on taxable income for the current tax year under three options:

1. Payments according to Revenue Canada's billing notices (no interest is charged if there is a shortfall at April 30).
2. Payments based on the prior year tax liability only (interest will be charged if there is a balance due at April 30).
3. Payments based on an estimate of current year tax liability (interest will be charged again if there is a shortfall on April 30).

Because of this prepayment requirement, which is based on each individual's tax liability, it is important to plan RRSP and RRIF withdrawals, adjust withholding tax on private pensions, understand the tax reporting for receipt of interest payments, and how to split income with your spouse, in order to avoid or reduce the payment of the quarterly tax instalment amounts.

191 STAY UNDER THE $2,000 INSTALMENT PAYMENT THRESHOLD

Those who do not have any, or enough, tax remitted at source will be required to remit income taxes by instalment four times each year: March 15, June 15, September 15 and December 15. (Farmers may continue to remit once a year on December 31.)

Information from the immediately prior year tax return and the two preceding tax years will be used to determine whether an individual will be required to make quarterly instalment payments. You will be required to remit to the federal government if the difference between tax payable and amounts withheld at source is greater than $2,000 in both the current year and either of the two preceding years.

The tax payable will include both the combined federal and provincial income taxes. Late or deficient instalment payments will be subject to an interest penalty, which has recently been increased to the rate charged on treasury bills of the last quarter, plus 4%. Be sure your tax-withholding arrangements keep you out of the instalment profile, or be prepared to prepay your taxes on a quarterly basis.

192 DECREASE INSTALMENT PAYMENTS AND INCREASE CASH FLOW

Don't overpay your instalment remittances when you could be investing or otherwise using your precious resources.

You can request that your instalment payment billings be reduced if your income clearly will be below that of the previous tax year. This could happen if you will be applying capital losses to capital gains this year, or if your income otherwise decreased over the previous years. Or, you can plan to reduce your same-level income by making a Spousal RRSP contribution, if possible, or by splitting Canada Pension Plan benefits with your spouse.

To lessen your burden at tax time, you can request that more tax be withheld from your monthly Old Age Security, Canada Pension Plan, or private pension cheque. However, this option will reduce your monthly cash flow.

You might also consider changing your asset mix. As you know, the accrued gains in equity-based investments are not taxed until dispositions. Also, dividends and capital gains income is taxed at lower marginal tax rates than pensions and interest. Therefore, it is possible to preserve your capital by managing your investments in such a way as to reduce the quarterly withdrawal of funds used to prepay your taxes. Speak to your tax and investment advisor about this.

193 OFFSET INTEREST CHARGES BY PREPAYING YOUR INSTALMENTS

Winter travellers may offset Revenue Canada interest charges on instalment remittances by prepaying their instalments before they leave. Alternatively, Revenue Canada can be given the required payments in post-dated cheques. If you mistakenly underpay your instalments, you can avoid interest charges by overpaying your next instalment to offset the deficiency.

Should your investment and other income sources drop due to economic conditions, you may request that a change be made to your current remittance method to an estimate of taxes payable for the current year, so that you can reduce your instalment remittance requirements altogether.

This is a good reason to monitor your income level throughout the year so as to minimize the amount you must prepay to the tax department.

194 UNDUE HARDSHIP MAY AFFECT YOUR OAS INCOME

Old Age Security pension payments (OAS) are received by those who turn age 65 during the year and are reported as taxable income and subject to a "Clawback" calculation. Each individual, whose net income exceeds $53,215, will have a withholding tax applied to Old Age Security cheques starting in July each year, based on income reported on the immediately prior tax year.

Every tax filing year, the clawback tax withheld will be credited to the liabilities otherwise payable and the new clawback will be prepared. It is therefore important to arrange your tax affairs so as to report the lowest net income possible. This will have a direct affect on your monthly income from the OAS.

Canadian residents will continue to receive their OAS cheques even if no tax return has been filed, unless they have ignored a Demand to File by the Minister, in which case the payments will stop. Non-residents are not as lucky. If they fail to file their prescribed form, the full amount of OAS will be withheld.

Revenue Canada may ignore the withholding tax on OAS if you can successfully plead undue hardship. This may happen, for example, if your income decreases sharply between the base tax year and the year of receipt. In such cases, contact your Tax Services Office to apply for tax relief.

As mentioned in the previous chapter, by the year 2001, the OAS will be replaced by the new tax free Seniors Benefit. Those who turned age 60 by December 31, 1995, have the option of staying with the current OAS system (which will, however, be modified because of the removal of the Age Credit and the Pension Income Amount in the same year). It is important to plan now for the most advantageous public pension option, as well as how investment opportunities and decisions can make up for any additional taxes dues to these changes.

195 COMPUTE YOUR AGE AMOUNT AT 65

At the age of 65 taxpayers will not only qualify for their Old Age Security Pension, as explained above, but in addition, they will calculate whether they are eligible to claim a new non-refundable tax credit: the Age Amount. This may be claimable if the taxpayer reached age 65 during the year, and has income within certain thresholds. The Age Amount is a maximum non-refundable tax credit of $3,482.

In the case of married couples, the higher-income earner can transfer the Age Amount of the spouse to his or her own tax return by using Schedule 2, if the lower-income earner does not need all of the credits to reduce taxes payable. This is a lucrative figure that can save you hundreds of dollars.

When one spouse dies, the OAS for that person stops. Also, in the year of death, the Age Amount is not allowed unless the taxpayer reached age 65 before the date of death. It is therefore important to plan for the potential changes in your tax-filing profile due to the loss of one spouse.

196 EVEN YOUR AGE AMOUNT CAN BE RESTRICTED

If you earn more than $25,921 in "net income" from pensions, investments or other sources, the Age Amount you would otherwise be entitled to will be reduced by 15% of any income over $25,921, to a maximum of $3,482 in 1995 and subsequent years.

When you factor in provincial taxes, this new tax provision could cost you up to 27% of the Age Amount or up to approximately $940 more, if your income wipes out the Age Credit completely. In addition, the restriction and its resulting tax liability could affect how much you'll pay on your quarterly tax instalment plan. Therefore it is important to prepare some preliminary tax calculations before year end, to see just how you will be affected by the Age Amount Restriction.

197 SPLIT THE CPP BENEFITS BETWEEN SPOUSES

One way to avoid clawbacks and reduce instalment tax payments is to split income sources between the two spouses. Many taxpayers are unaware that effective January 1, 1987, rights to Canada Pension Plan retirement benefits may be assigned to a spouse, including a common-law spouse. This is an excellent way of splitting the reporting of the CPP retirement income between spouses. For the purpose of income splitting, the benefits must be retirement benefits, and either a single or double assignment of benefits may be made.

Under a single assignment, only one spouse has applied for or is receiving the CPP retirement benefits. The other spouse will not have previously made CPP contributions, and must be at least 60 years of age. The result of assignment is that part of the pension received by the contributor is paid to, and therefore reported by, each spouse on the tax return.

Under a double assignment, both spouses will be eligible to receive or are receiving CPP retirement benefits, but total benefits received by both will be distributed evenly. Total pensions payable to each individual will be split; that is, it is not possible to split only one spouse's CPP retirement pension. The amount that is split between spouses is calculated as 50% of the number of months in the marriage, divided by the number of months in the contributory period (starting from age 18 or January 1966). Retirement benefits from CPP do not qualify as "earned income for RRSP purposes." Work out your returns both ways — with the CPP Spousal Split and without it — to determine the best tax position.

198 CALCULATE THE CPP BENEFITS PRORATION

New in '97

In the year a taxpayer starts receiving benefits from CPP, there is no longer a requirement to contribute premiums to the plan through employment or self-employment. Therefore, any CPP premium amounts paid after the month in which the taxpayer starts to collect CPP benefits, will result in an overpayment, which can be applied for when you file your tax return. This same rule holds true in the year of death, when premiums need only be paid up to the date of death, or in the year *a taxpayer turns 70,* when no premiums are required after this month.

Remember, in 1997 an extra adjustment will have to be computed for the shortfall in withholding for Canada Pension Plan premiums by employers, due to the increase in CPP premium rates midway through the year.

199 CREATE RRSP ROOM WITH CPP DISABILITY BENEFITS

Effective on amounts received after 1990, CPP disability benefits have qualified and will continue to qualify as earned income for RRSP purposes.

This means that 18% of the CPP disability benefits received in the prior year can be contributed to an RRSP and used to reduce your tax liability, provided you are not restricted from doing so because of your age.

200 SPLIT THE REPORTING OF CPP LUMP SUM PAYMENTS

It is quite common for a taxpayer to have to wait months, and often years, to receive a CPP disability amount, with the result that a retroactive lump sum can be received in one tax year. The part of the benefit that relates to years other than the current tax year is automatically applied to the prior years by Revenue Canada if it exceeds $300.

Report the full amount on the T4A(P) on the current year's tax return. Revenue Canada will then adjust the return. When the true net income of the recipient of the CPP disability pension is known, go back to adjust the spouse's return for a possible Spousal Amount, medical expenses, charitable donations or political contributions transfer, if these changes give the family unit a better tax benefit.

Starting in 1996, all lump sums received from the CPP will qualify for this application of benefits to prior years, including Death Benefits, which might not be received until the tax year after the year of death. Request adjustment to prior-filed returns for this special tax treatment, if you have such income amounts in 1996 or 1997.

201 KNOW WHAT INCOME QUALIFIES FOR THE PENSION INCOME AMOUNT

The $1,000 pension income amount on line 314 of the tax return is available to certain taxpayers, depending on age and source of pension income received. The rules for claiming it are as follows:

If the taxpayer is over age 64 and in receipt of the following, the $1,000 pension income amount applies to offset:

(a) pension payments received from a superannuation pension plan as part of a life annuity;

(b) payments from a Registered Retirement Income Fund;

(c) annuity payments from a Deferred Profit Sharing Plan;

(d) taxable portion of other annuities, including earnings from foreign sources, less any amount deducted at line 256;

(e) annuity payments from an Income Averaging Annuity Contract (IAAC);

(f) amounts from Box 16 of a T4RSP/RIF Slip (annuity payments).

If the taxpayer is under age 65, the $1,000 pension income amount also applies to offset the following income sources:

- pension payments received from a pension plan as a life annuity, less any amounts transferred as a spousal RRSP
- amounts listed in (b) to (f) above if received as a result of the spouse's death.

INELIGIBLE PENSION INCOME SOURCES for the $1,000 pension credit include:

- Old Age Security and supplements
- Spouse's Allowances
- Canada Pension Plan benefits
- Retirement Compensation Arrangements
- employment benefit plans
- employee trust or prescribed provincial pension plans (Saskatchewan Pension Plan)
- death benefits
- lump-sum payments on withdrawal of a pension fund
- Deferred Profit Sharing Plan or Registered Pension Plan payments transferred to an RRSP
- retiring allowances such as severance pay
- salary deferral arrangements.

BONUS TIPS

202 DON'T FORGET TO CLAIM YOUR MEDICAL EXPENSES

One of the most lucrative yet most commonly missed tax credits for uninsured taxpayers is the medical expenses credit, its new partner, the new Refundable Medical Expense Supplement, as well as its associate, the Disability Tax Credit.

First, it is important for those who pay any amounts towards medical expenses or health insurance plans to claim medical expenses on the tax return as a non-refundable tax credit. This includes the expenses of the taxpayer or spouse and dependants for any 12-month period ending in the tax year that is in excess of 3% of net income. (The 3% limitation has been restricted to a maximum of $1,614 since 1992.) Because of this restriction, it is usually more effective to claim the medical expenses on the tax return of the person with the lower net income. This is particularly important with the introduction of the Refundable Medical

Expenses Supplement. In the case of a deceased taxpayer, expenses may be included for any 24-month period including the date of death.

Medical expenses are not restricted to those incurred or paid in Canada, but they must have been paid on behalf of a Canadian resident or deemed resident. Starting in 1996, supporting individuals only claim the medical expense tax credit for qualifying expenses incurred on behalf of a dependent spouse, child, grandchild, parent, grandparent, brother, sister, uncle, aunt, niece, or nephew. In addition, starting in 1997, up to $10,000 in full or part-time home attendant care costs for those with a prolonged mental or physical impairment may be claimed as a medical expense. In the year of death, this amount increases to $20,000.

Be sure to file for your medical expenses on the T1 General return, but reduce them by any reimbursements received from health insurance plans. You can also go back and recover missed credits of prior years by requesting an adjustment to your prior tax returns all the way back to 1985.

✸ 203 LIST ALL MEDICAL EXPENDITURES THAT ARE TAX DEDUCTIBLE

New in '97

One of the most commonly missed medical expenses is Blue Cross or other private health care plan premiums. The following list of expenses gives other common items often missed on the tax return:

Type of Expense	Description
Medical Practitioner	Dentists, doctors, nurses, osteopaths, chiropractors, naturopaths, therapists, podiatrists, optometrists, psychiatrists, psychologists, speech therapists, Christian Science practitioners.
Payments to Societies	Physiotherapists employed by Arthritis Society and Associations, Victorian Order of Nurses, Canadian Mothercraft Society.
Private Hospitals	Possession of municipal licence designating institution as a hospital is necessary. Respite care costs of up to $5,000 will be deductible as well.
Attendants	For full-time care of person in nursing home; care in a self-contained domestic establishment; accompanying patient in travelling for medical treatment (costs of board and lodging).
Institutions	Costs for care and/or training of physically or mentally disabled person, including persons suffering from behavioural problems and attendance problems. Rehabilitative therapy, including training in sign language

	and lip reading are also allowed beginning in 1992 and for future years.

Services   Payments for sign language interpretation provided to someone who has a speech or hearing impairment, if the fees are paid to a person engaged in the business of providing such services; reasonable moving expenses (up to a maximum of $2,000) of an individual who lacks normal physical development or who has a severe and prolonged mobility impairment, to a place that is more accessible; reasonable costs of alteration to the driveway of an individual's residence in order to facilitate access to a bus; amounts that are not in excess of $5,000 and/or equal to 20% of the cost of a van that has been adapted for a person who uses a wheelchair at the time of purchase or within 6 months of purchase.

Transportation and Travel Costs   By ambulance for a patient, paid to a person who is employed in providing such transportation services; costs for use of vehicle (land, air or water) owned by taxpayer or family member as well as other expenses of transporting one accompanying individual if the patient is certified to require an attendant. Such reasonable travel expenses are allowed only if patient and attendant must travel 80 km or more to receive medical services not available in locality; also allowed if patient travels alone; reasonable expenses must be verified by receipts.

204   CALCULATE THE NEW REFUNDABLE MEDICAL EXPENSE SUPPLEMENT

Starting with the 1997 tax filing year, a new refundable medical expense supplement is available to those individuals whose "adjusted" income meets certain thresholds. The eligible individual is someone who is 18 years of age or older at the end of the year and whose total business and employment income (excluding disability benefits) is at least $2500. This "adjusted income" figure is also defined as being the income of the individual and that of his/her spouse.

The credit is equal to the lesser of $500 and 25% of the medical expense credit claimed elsewhere on the tax return for the year. This supplement is then reduced by 5% of the net family income over $16,069 in 1997. It is eliminated when net family income exceeds $26,069. These amounts will be indexed in future years.

Therefore, to maximize your claim under this new provision it is important to include all medical expenses incurred, to choose the best

12-month period ending in the tax year to maximize your claim (you might be able to reach back and include some unclaimed expenses from last year) and then to claim these amounts on the return of the person with the lower net income to benefit the most from the 3% net income limitation, and this new refundable tax credit.

205 BE AWARE OF DISABILITY CREDIT ELIGIBILITY CRITERIA

Those who suffer from a severe and prolonged medical impairment may claim a special tax credit on the tax return, or if not taxable, may transfer it to their supporting individuals. To qualify, a doctor must verify the nature of the infirmity following strict guidelines set out by Revenue Canada:

A prolonged impairment is one that has lasted for at least 12 continuous months ending in the tax year or has begun in the tax year and is expected to last at least 12 continuous months. A severe impairment is one that, on a prolonged basis, markedly restricts all or substantially all of the time (90% or more) a person's ability to perform basic activities of daily living.

A marked restriction is one that causes the person to be unable to perform basic activities of daily living even with the use of appropriate devices, medication or therapy or causes the person to take an excessive amount of time to perform basic activities of daily living. Persons with permanent visual impairment (legal blindness) qualify for the tax credit.

In the case of children with disabilities, the child's developmental progress in relation to the norm and the prognosis of the condition as it affects the child's ability to perform basic activities of daily living are taken into consideration.

Basic activities of daily living are defined as (a) feeding and dressing oneself; (b) eliminating (bowel and bladder functions); (c) walking; (d) speaking, so as to be understood by a person who knows him in a quiet setting; (e) hearing, so that the person can understand a conversation with a familiar person in a quiet setting; (f) cognitive functions (perceiving, thinking and remembering).

For the purposes of claiming this credit, basic activities of daily living do not include working, recreation, housekeeping or social activities.

Obtain Form T2201 Disability Credit Certificate, and have your doctor sign it. This credit may be claimed by a supporting individual for severely disabled dependent grandchildren, parents, and grandparents starting in the 1996 and future years, as well as for dependent children and spouses.

206 FILE BACK TO RECOVER MISSED DISABILITY TAX CREDITS

Usually, the onset of a disability in the family is a stressful event. The tax consequences of the disability are often forgotten. Fortunately, the disability credit can be recovered by requesting an adjustment to a prior-filed return. If your loved one suffered from any of the following afflictions, you may still be able to claim this lucrative tax credit:

- legal blindness (20/200 or less) or severe macular degeneration
- mobility: confinement to a bed or wheelchair for a substantial part of the day or severe arthritis involving multiple major joints
- communication: profound bilateral deafness, expressive and sensory aphasia, speech impairment
- mental functions: supervision required in self-care activities including dressing, feeding, bathing and eating
- cardio-respiratory systems: dyspnea or angina while performing basic living activities
- neurological systems: severe epilepsy, severe ataxia, bowel or bladder incontinence, marked decrease in mentation, marked dysarthia
- genito-urinary system: persons disabled despite receiving peritonal dialysis; person with renal failure needing 23 or more hours a week of haemodialysis
- endocrine system: diabetes mellitus that causes peripheral vascular insufficiency
- multiple body systems: including pulmonary, gastrointestinal or central nervous systems
- cancer: related to the severity and effect of the cancer on ability to perform basic activities.

The credit ($4,233) is worth close to $1,200 each year. Recouping missed Disability Credits can go a long way in helping a family during difficult times.

207 TRANSFER ELIGIBLE TAX CREDITS BETWEEN SPOUSES

Four different provisions on the tax return may be transferred between spouses, including common-law spouses. They are:
- Pension Income Amount
- Age Amount
- Disability Amount

• Tuition and Education Amount (up to $5,000 in tuition fees or education credits).

If your spouse is not taxable, or does not need all of the credits listed above to reduce income taxes to zero, transfer the unused portions of his or her tax credits to your return to reap bonus tax benefits. To do so, complete Schedule 2.

208 GROUP TAX CREDITS ON ONE RETURN TO MAXIMIZE FAMILY TAX BENEFITS

As a general policy, Revenue Canada allows a husband and wife (including a common-law spouse) to group certain expenditures—medical expenses, charitable donations and political contributions — paid by each individual spouse on one tax return to maximize tax benefits.

For example, medical expenses should be combined and claimed on the return of the lower taxable income earner to maximize the 3% of net income limitation. Donations, on the other hand, should usually be grouped and claimed by the higher-income earner, to maximize the use of the 75% of net income limitation, effective the 1997 and future tax years.

Political contributions should also be grouped and claimed by the higher earner, up to a maximum contribution of $1150 (which equals the $500 credit allowed).

Your goal is to file your returns in such a way as to pay the least amount of taxes possible as a family unit.

CONCLUSION

At The Jacks Institute, when we teach income tax preparation to Canadians across the country, we believe in what we call the "Best Benefit Theory":

"It is not good enough simply to compute the tax return mathematically correctly: be sure you have claimed all deductions, credits and tax planning benefits your family is entitled to."

These tax tips are written to help you recognize tax savers when they arise in response to different circumstances in your life. I hope you have found them enlightening, that they will help you seek out qualified professional help when needed, and that they will ultimately save you and your family money.

Many happy returns,
Evelyn Jacks

CHAPTER 11

32 COMMON TAX FILING TRAPS

The following are common tax filing traps you might fall into when you prepare your tax return. Watch out for them and save extra money!

INCOME REPORTING

1. *Missing T4 Slips:* Even casual employment is taxable as are tips and gratuities and employment for which no T4 Slip was received. In such cases, estimate income and source deductions, using your pay stubs. In the case of service industry employees, keep a daily log of all tips earned, to breeze through a tax audit.

2. *Missing Interest Income:* Financial institutions will not send out a T5 Slip if interest earnings are less than $50; so check bank books for this information. Don't forget to claim interest Revenue Canada may have paid you.

3. *Double-Reported Interest:* If you have pre-reported interest on compounding investments such as Canada Savings Bonds or Guaranteed Investment Certificates, be sure to subtract any such amounts from the total income you receive in the year you cash the investment.

4. *Over-Reported Scholarship Income:* Claim a $500 exemption on any income received during the year from scholarships, fellowships and bursaries.

5. *Over-Reported Alimony Income:* If you have received a lump sum settlement on the occasion of your marital break-up, the amount is tax free to the recipient and not deductible by the payor. And remember that for agreements negotiated or changed after April 30, 1997, child support will no longer be taxable to the recipient or tax deductible to the payor.

6. *Over-reported Income From Social Benefits:* You will be required to report any amounts received from Social Assistance, Workers' Compensation or Federal Old Age Supplements on the tax return, even though these amounts are not taxable. The amounts will be used, however, to decrease refundable tax credits otherwise payable to you. Be sure to take the offsetting deduction for these amounts on Line 250.

7. *Under-Reported Business Income:* Be sure to report all business income received in the fiscal year. Those proprietorships that switched their non-calendar fiscal year ends to December 31 in 1995, must be careful to compute income earned this year by taking into account the 10-year reserve provisions. Remember, a transitional reserve can be claimed to reduce the impact of the additional taxes generated by this one time adjustment. An alternative calculation is available to those who elected to retain their non-calendar fiscal year ends (see Form T1139).

8. *Report Foreign Holdings:* For 1997 and future tax years, it will be necessary to disclose dealings with foreign trusts and affiliates, or face penalty provisions. Be sure to keep relevant documentaion.

9. *Average CPP Lump Sum Payments:* Remember that new tax treatment will apply to lump sums received from the CPP, so wait for the Notice of Assessment to check the computation and transfer of all relevant tax provisions available to the family.

CLAIMING OF DEDUCTIONS

10. *Under-Utilized RRSP Contributions:* Maximize your allowable RRSP contribution room to reduce net income, which will in turn increase other provisions available, such as the Child Tax Benefit, the Goods and Services Tax Credit, the Refundable Medical Expense Supplement, and provincial tax credits.

11. *Under-Claimed Child Care Expenses:* While child care is usually claimed by the lower-income earner, the higher earner can take a limited deduction if the spouse was attending full time at a designated educational institute, or was hospitalized or incarcerated for at least two weeks in the year. Obtain Form T778. Remember, for parents who attend school there is a special new child care calculation for 1996 and future years.

12. *Under-Reported Moving Expenses:* Keep all receipts, then claim costs of all removal expenses for yourself and your family, provided you have moved at least 40 kilometres closer to a new

work or self-employment location. These deductions include temporary living accommodations for up to 15 days at the new location, real estate commissions paid to sell the house at the old location and removal expenses for the household effects and family members. However, to qualify there must be employment, self-employment or scholarship income at the new location.

13. *Missing Alimony or Maintenance Deductions:* Claim the periodic payments you make to your ex-spouse and children as per your written agreement, judgment or court order for the current year, and the immediately preceding year, if the agreement was made prior to May 1, 1997. If you were a recipient of such payments, and were required to repay some or all of them, claim a deduction for any amounts previously included in income. However, tax changes will allow child support to be received on a tax-free basis, but at the expense of the payor, who will lose his/her tax deduction, for agreements made or changed after April 30, 1997.

14. *Missed Carrying Charges:* Claim the costs of your Safety Deposit Box, investment accounting fees, and interest paid on investment loans (for non-registered investments including charges for purchasing Canada Savings Bonds on a payroll plan). But remember that the administration fees for your RRSP will no longer be tax deductible after 1995. RESP fees are no longer deductible after 1997.

15. *Unclaimed Employment Expenses:* Don't forget to claim auto, travel, cost of supplies or in the case of commission salespeople, entertainment and promotion, if you are required by your contract of employment to pay these amounts out of your own pocket. Your employer must sign Form T2200 to verify that all required conditions are met in order for you to make this claim.

16. *Legal Expenses:* While you cannot claim the cost of your legal fees paid to obtain a divorce or separation, you can claim the costs of enforcing payments already established by the courts.

17. *Capital Gains Exemption:* Don't forget that the $500,000 Super Exemption is still with us and available to you should you sell qualified small business corporation shares or qualified farm property.

18. *Northern Residents' Deductions:* A special deduction may be made if you have lived in a "prescribed northern zone" or a "prescribed intermediate zone" for six consecutive months or more during the year. Obtain a copy of Revenue Canada's Northern Residents' Guide.

CLAIMING OF NON-REFUNDABLE TAX CREDITS

19. *Missing the Restrictions on Claiming the Age Amount:* Since 1994, the Age Amount has been restricted in cases where net income exceeds $25,921. Be sure to make the calculation or you could owe Revenue Canada more after you file your return.

20. *Equivalent-to-Spouse Amount:* If you are a single parent, who is not living common law, and you are solely supporting your child, parent or grandparent, a non-refundable tax credit may be available to you, depending on the level of your dependant's income, calculated in the same manner as the Spousal Amount.

21. *Over or Under-Contributions to the Canada Pension Plan:* It is possible if you had more than one employer, that you have over-contributed your CPP premiums. Or, if you turned 18, the age of 70, started to receive CPP retirement benefits, or in the year of death, premiums are only required for a portion of the year. File Form T2204 with your tax return to make the calculations. Make the special adjustment to premiums payable into the CPP for the 1997 tax year. Your employer will probably have under-contributed these premiums by .075% in 1997.

22. *Pension Income Amount:* Those who receive periodic pension payments from a company pension plan may claim a maximum of $1,000 under the pension income amount to offset net income, regardless of age. The credit is also allowed for annuity payments under certain plans such as a RRIF or other annuities if you are over age 65, or receiving the amounts as a result of your spouse's death.

23. *Tuition Fees:* If you are attending a designated post-secondary educational institute, including one certified by Human Resources Development Canada in providing occupational skills, a non-refundable tax credit is claimable if amounts exceed $100, and the taxpayer is at least 16 years old. Tuition fees are claimable for amounts expended for sessions held during the calendar year only. Remember that you can now carry forward such amounts, if not needed to reduce taxable income or if there is no one to whom the amounts can be transferred.

24. *Education Credit:* Claim $150 a month for each month you were in full-time attendance at a designated educational institute during the calendar year. (Part-time attendance qualifies if you are disabled.) Again the amounts may be carried forward to future years, if this is more advantageous to you.

25. *Transfer of Tuition/Education Amounts:* Transfer up to $5,000 of these two amounts to your supporting parent, grandparent, spouse, or legal guardian...but transfer only what's needed to reduce their income; the rest can be carried forward by the student.

26. *Claim All Medical Expenses:* Medical expenses such as Blue Cross or other private health insurance premiums are claimable for the best 12-month period ending in the tax year. Also be sure to claim glasses, dental work, hearing aids and their batteries, prescription drugs, and even travelling expenses for prescribed medical treatments not available in your home community. Receipts are required. Don't forget to use these medical claims in the computation of the Refundable Medical Expense Supplement available for the 1997 and future tax years.

27. *Couple-Up on Charities:* Revenue Canada will allow spouses to claim each other's charitable donations. It is better to do so on the return of the higher-income earner to maximize the two-tier credit structure. You can also "save" the donations and group them for one claim in a period of up to five years, provided they are never claimed twice. Remember though, generally the claim may not exceed 75% of your net income in any one tax year, or 100% of net income in the year of death or the immediately preceding year.

SPECIAL PROVISIONS

28. *Political Contributions:* Significant political contribution credits of up to $500 may be claimed against federal taxes payable, and in some provinces, against provincial taxes.

29. *Labour-Sponsored Venture Capital Tax Credits:* A federal tax credit of up to $525 may be claimed for these RRSP-eligible investments. Many provinces also match this credit against provincial taxes payable.

30. *GST/HST Rebate:* Be sure to make a claim for the GST/HST Rebate any time you claimed expenses from employment or a partnership in line 212 or 229 of the tax return.

31. *Instalment Payments:* Don't forget to dig out documentation for the quarterly instalment payments you made during the year, to offset the taxes payable on your tax return.

32. *Know Your Tax Filing Methods:* You can file your return on paper, or electronically, using a third-party transmitter. Contact Revenue Canada for a list of EFILE agents in your area, to speed up the processing of your tax return.

CHAPTER 12

20 TIPS FOR YEAR END TAX PLANNING

1. *KNOW YOUR TAX FILING RIGHTS:* Every Canadian has the right to arrange his or her affairs within the framework of the law so as to pay the least amount of income taxes possible. To identify and take advantage of all your options, set aside some time at year end to analyze your current year's income and expense records and your current financial portfolio. It could pay off at tax time.

2. *DETERMINE YOUR FAMILY'S TAX FILING PORTFOLIO:* List all major financial and personal events that occurred in the current tax year. In the process, dig out last year's returns to see if you missed filing for a lucrative tax deduction or credit. If you have still not filed a prior year's return, doing so now could result in a nice tax refund in time for Christmas, or at very least, some extra RRSP contribution room.

3. *FILE ADJUSTMENTS FOR MISSED TAX PROVISIONS:* When you've found prior errors, correct them by filing a letter with your Tax Services Office to claim your overpaid taxes. Every penny counts! You may go back to tax year 1985 to request changes for most provisions.

4. *LIST ALL MISSING INFORMATION:* Do you wish to consult with your broker before year end? Give to your favourite charity? Claim home office expenses for the first time, order new forms from Revenue Canada? Make a list of information to gather, including a mortgage interest statement from your financial institution, duplicate receipts for prior years or auto expense log books.

5. *SORT MEDICAL EXPENSES BEFORE YEAR END:* Sort these in chronological order and be sure to carry forward any unused receipts from last year. Create a "fiscal year" with at least one month in the 12-month period ending in the current tax year. This may create a better claim for you than the calendar year and help you recover some tax benefits from last year's expenses. Remember to reduce all medical expenses by any reimbursements from your medical plans and the total, by 3% of your net income to a maximum of $1,614. Also remember that this effort might pay off in the creation of the New Refundable Medical Expense Supplement.

6. *GIVE TO YOUR FAVOURITE CHARITY BEFORE YEAR END:* If you give, by December 31 of the current year, the charitable donations you anticipate giving early in the new year, you'll speed up your tax benefits by filing them on the tax return for the current tax year this spring. Otherwise you'll have to wait to file next year's return to reap any rewards.

7. *CONSIDER POLITICAL CONTRIBUTIONS AS A TAX BENEFIT:* By giving to your favourite political party by December 31, you receive a tax credit of $75 for the first $100 you give. A maximum credit of $500 can be claimed as a result of a contribution of $1,150. Both federal and provincial credits are available.

8. *PLAN ASSET DISPOSITIONS CAREFULLY:* Review your potential capital gains and losses for the current tax year before generating them with dispositions. In general, capital losses can only be applied to capital gains of the year, not other income sources. However, you can choose to bring forward any previously unapplied capital losses to reduce capital gains you may be reporting, as an alternative to selling existing assets at a loss.

9. *PURCHASE CAPITAL ASSETS:* For proprietors, late-year asset purchases can create capital cost allowance claims of one-half of the usual allowable rates. In the year of acquisition, you can receive a 30% write-off on half the acquisition costs of a new computer purchase, for example, or a new vehicle that was purchased before the end of the year.

10. *REDUCE TAX ON PENSION INCOME:* If you are receiving periodic pension benefits from any pension sources, be sure to maximize your allowable deductions for carrying charges, RRSP contribution room, or to charities, in order to reduce the tax you must pay, and keep more of your Old Age Security and offsetting Age Amount.

11. *PLAN INTER-PROVINCIAL MOVES CAREFULLY:* If you are changing province of residence, your income for the whole year will be taxed at the provincial rate applicable to your province of residence on December 31. A permanent move to Alberta from Ontario, for example, should be contemplated before year end. Income for the whole year will then be taxed at the lower Alberta rates, resulting in a bigger tax refund. However, if you'll be moving from Alberta to Saskatchewan, consider spending New Year's in the mountains. A move early in the new year will save tax dollars on this year's return.

12. *INCUR OPERATIONAL EXPENSES BEFORE YEAR END:* Sole proprietors and individual partners with a December 31 year end or certain commissioned salespersons who are eligible to claim expenses against their employment income, should consider making the following expenditures: fill up the gas tank, repair the car, purchase office supplies, install that business phone or fax line, or distribute those promotional flyers. Doing so before the year end will accelerate the tax benefits.

13. *KEEP AN AUTO LOG:* Make a resolution to record all business and personal driving during the year to maximize your claim for auto expenses. This is a simple procedure that will save you money during a tax audit.

14. *LOG UNRECEIPTED EXPENSES:* Don't forget to claim reasonable expenses for unreceipted amounts paid to wash your car at a coin car wash, for parking or for coin telephone calls.

15. *KEEP TIME CARDS FOR PAYING YOUR CHILDREN:* Commissioned salespeople and proprietors can claim the amounts paid to family members who have worked in the family business, provided proper documentation is kept and the work is actually performed at a rate you would normally pay a stranger.

16. *DON'T FILE ON THE WRONG TAX RETURN:* Only the T1 General makes reference to all the tax deductions and credits you may be entitled to. Short forms may be simpler, but could cost you money in the long run. Plan to obtain the right return for your tax filing profile.

17. *GET YOUR REFUND MORE QUICKLY USING DIRECT DEPOSIT:* To get the quickest possible refund, file form T1-DD and request that your refund cheque be deposited directly to your bank account. The same arrangement can also be made for

your Child Tax Benefit payments and the GST Credits. You may wish to change these arrangements in the new tax filing year.

18. *KEEP ALL PAPER DOCUMENTATION:* You must retain paper records supporting the figures on your tax return for a period of at least six years from the end on the year in which you receive your Notice of Assessment. If Revenue Canada requests a review, you must produce these, or your tax deductions will be disallowed.

19. *DO A PRELIMINARY TAX CALCULATION:* The earlier in the year you can run through a tax calculation for your family, the better your chances of maximizing your RRSP contributions to reduce your taxes payable. You'll also have several months to save up for a tax bill on April 30, and to lessen the stress you'll feel if you wait until the last minute.

20. *KNOW WHEN TO CONSULT A TAX PROFESSIONAL:* Everyone should attempt to understand his or her own tax return to make better "tax-wise" decisions during the year. However, a tax professional can help you save time and money in completing your return or in appealing an assessment from Revenue Canada. Always ask for an estimate and evidence of a guarantee before you engage this individual or firm for this most important task. It may pay off handsomely over the long run to have a knowledgeable tax professional at your side to guide you to tax savings.

Note: Revenue Canada tells us that the No. 1 error made by Canadians is still errors in math. Check your computations carefully, or consider using tax software to help with this annual task.

INDEX

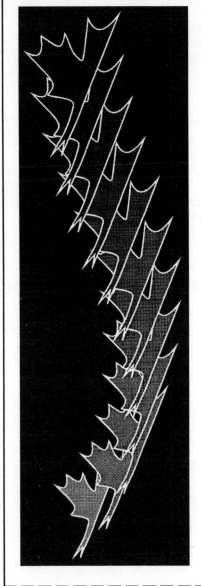

Free Bonus Offer!

Receive a free one-year subscription to

The Jacks Tax Update Newsletter

(retail value: $75.00)

The Jacks on Tax Update Newsletter provides quarterly updates on significant personal tax changes throughout the year.

To receive your free one-year subscription to *The Jacks on Tax Update Newsletter,* complete the form below and send/fax to:

> THE JACKS INSTITUTE
> Newsletter Subscription Offer
> 401-177 Lombard Avenue
> Winnipeg, Manitoba
> R3B 5W6
> Fax (204) 949-9429
>
> OR
>
> Call locally (204) 956-7161
> 1-800-563-3276 (Toll free)
>
> OR
> Email: tax@jackstax.com

❏ Please send me a free brochure about your tax courses

Name_____

Address _____

City _____ Prov _____ Code _____

Phone _____ Fax _____

One-Eyed Cat

之后，他开始想象她不在家的那几个月里，夜里他怎样在家里上下楼梯、进出所有屋子，也许还上阁楼的情景。

"这次是你来找我的。"他说。

"是的。我看见你朝枫树林那边走，就跟着你过来了。"

他们身后的门打开了，灯光照在他们身上，他们俩都站起来转过身。

爸爸正站在门口，大厅的灯开着。他身上穿了件浴袍，脚上穿着双旧皮拖鞋。

他用一只手挡住照在眼睛上的光线，往外看他们。

"你们在那儿呢！"他说着，笑了。"我一直在满屋子找你们呢。然后我就想，在春天这么美丽的夜晚，他们散步去了。"

"我们去梅克皮斯大厦了。"妈妈说。

"我真高兴你们回家了。"爸爸说道。

一只眼睛的猫

葆拉·福克斯
Paula Fox

　　葆拉·福克斯于1923年出生于纽约。在婴儿时期她便被父母遗弃,几经转手,在颠沛流离中度过懵懵懂懂的童年。正是这一独特的 "旅行式"经历,锻炼了葆拉独立生活的能力。她的一生干过很多职业,直到43岁成为教师之后才正式开始写作。最终与家人在希腊团聚时,葆拉创作了处女作小说《可怜的乔治》。随后,她创作了第一本面向儿童的作品《莫里斯的房间》。她的儿童作品成就引人瞩目,其中最有名的要数获得1974年纽伯瑞儿童文学奖的《月光之号》,以及1985年获纽伯瑞儿童文学奖的《一只眼睛的猫》。此外还有《石脸男孩》(1968)、《海里的河豚》(1970)等。